Wire Gauge Chart

This chart helps you determine the proper power-wire gauge when you know the fuse ratings of your amplifiers and their distance from the battery. For example, if your amplifier is drawing 60 amperes of current and the distance to the car's battery from the amplifiers is 12 feet, locate where the ampere rating along the top intersects with the approximate distance in the middle area of the chart, and then determine the proper wire gauge on the left. (In this example, it would be 8 gauge.)

Amperage	20	30	40	50	60	75	100	150	200	500	750
00							57	38	29	11	8
0						61	45	30	23	9	6
1					60	48	36	24	18	7	X
2				57	48	38	29	19	14	X	X
3			57	45	38	30	23	15	11	X	X
4		60	45	36	30	24	18	12	9	X	X
5	71	48	36	29	24	19	14	10	7	X	X
6	57	38	28	23	19	15	11	8	X	X	X
7	45	30	22	18	15	12	9	X	X	X	X
8	36	24	18	14	12	9	X	X	X	X	X
9	28	19	14	11	9	X	X	X	X	X	X
10	22	15	11	9	X	X	X	X	X	X	X
12	14	9	7	X	X	X	X	X	X	X	X

Wire Gauge (vertical axis label)

Chart courtesy of IASCA.

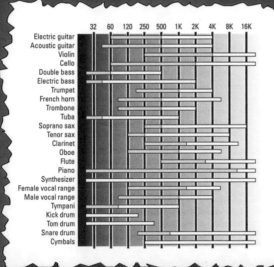

Frequency Range of Common Musical Instruments

This graph illustrates the frequency range of many common musical instruments to give you an idea of the frequency range a car audio system will need to reproduce to accurately re-create the sound of these instruments.

Signal Flow Diagram of a Car Audio System

This figure shows the architecture of a common car audio system. The dotted black line shows the path of the preamp audio signal (before it's amplified), from a head unit, through an equalizer and electronic crossover and to the amplifier. A video signal is also sent from the head unit to a pair of video screens in the back seat area. From the amplifier, an amplified audio signal (the solid black line) goes to each speaker in the system. One amplifier powers a subwoofer. The other amplifier powers a set of component speakers in the front of the car (with the signal first passing through the speakers' passive crossovers) and a pair of coaxial speakers in the rear of the car. The gray line shows power flowing through a power cable from the car's battery to the amplifiers, and the power cable is protected by an in-line fuse.

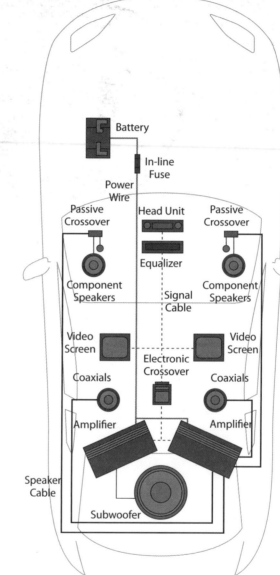

Car Audio

FOR

DUMMIES®

Car Audio
FOR
DUMMIES®

by Doug Newcomb

Foreword by Mike Mettler
Vice President/Editor-In-Chief, *Sound & Vision* magazine

WILEY

Wiley Publishing, Inc.

Car Audio For Dummies®

Published by
Wiley Publishing, Inc.
111 River Street
Hoboken, NJ 07030-5774

www.wiley.com

Copyright © 2008 by Wiley Publishing, Inc., Indianapolis, Indiana

Published by Wiley Publishing, Inc., Indianapolis, Indiana

Published simultaneously in Canada

For general information on our other products and services, please contact our Customer Care Department within the U.S. at 800-762-2974, outside the U.S. at 317-572-3993, or fax 317-572-4002.

For technical support, please visit www.wiley.com/techsupport.

Wiley also publishes its books in a variety of electronic formats. Some content that appears in print may not be available in electronic books.

Library of Congress Control Number: 2007942526

ISBN: 978-0-470-15158-7

Manufactured in the United States of America

10 9 8 7 6 5 4 3 2 1

WILEY

About the Author

Doug Newcomb has been writing about car audio since 1988. He was editor of the trade magazine *Installation News* (now called *Mobile Electronics*) from 1988 to 1989 and managing editor of *Car Audio and Electronics* magazine from 1989 to 1995, and editor from 1995 to 1997. He served as executive editor for *Car Stereo Review*, which became *Mobile Entertainment,* and then *Road & Track Road Gear*, from 1997 to 2005.

As a freelance writer, Doug's work has appeared in numerous national publications, including *Rolling Stone, Playboy, Men's Journal,* and *Road & Track*. Doug has appeared on national television several times as an expert on in-car electronics, and he is frequently asked to speak at consumer electronics and automotive industry conventions as an authority on the subject.

Doug is currently a fulltime freelance writer whose work appears regularly in such publications as *Car Audio and Electronics, Sound & Vision, E-Gear,* and *SEMA News* and online for MSN Autos and MSN Tech & Gadgets.

Doug's love for music and cars started in the late 1970s when he installed his first stereo — a Craig eight-track tape player and two Sparkomatic 6x9s — in his first car, a 1968 Ford Fairlane. More than 30 years later, driving and listening to music is still one of his favorite activities.

He resides in Hood River, Oregon, with his wife and two children.

Dedication

I dedicate this book to my wife Gretchen, for her tireless support throughout this project, her always insightful advice, her eagle-eye proofreading, and for enduring all of those times over the years when I cranked the car stereo, even when she didn't like my "wiry" music. I would also like to thank my kids for their support and understanding during all those times when daddy was writing and couldn't play, and for sharing my love of cruising and listening to music. Finally, I'd like to acknowledge my parents, James and Ruby Newcomb, for teaching me the values and virtues of hard work.

A special dedication goes out to William "Bill" Burton for his unwavering editorial integrity and all he taught me about publishing, audio, and being human.

Author's Acknowledgments

Of the many people who helped with this book, some deserve special attention for going above and beyond the call of duty.

My lovely, talented, and infinitely patient wife Gretchen Newcomb gets more credit than I can ever repay for "midwifing" this project and holding up more than her fair share of household duties while I was writing this book.

Isaac "Iron Man" Goren of Sounds Good Stereo, Security and Marine in Woodland Hills, California, for all those hours on the phone explaining the finer points of car audio from a real-world perspective, and for being a great guy.

Micah "Voodoo" Sheveloff of WIRC Media Tactics for helping out with initial technical editing and being a good friend and sounding board.

Paul DiComo of Polk Audio and Definitive Technology for help with speaker information and being a great "uncle."

Stephen Witt of Alpine Electronics for all of those morning commute calls and always being there to help.

Tom and Martha Walker of AudioControl; Tom for help with technical editing and Martha for being a swift art whiz.

Derek Kenney of Sound in Motion in Boston for spending a Sunday afternoon on the phone with me explaining gain-setting and for all his help over the years.

Manville Smith of JL Audio for spending time helping me sort out subwoofer wiring schemes.

Kas Alves, Jerry Elliot, and Colin Ross at Scosche for their help.

I'd also like to thank Jennifer Quon of Alpine Electronics, Todd Goodnight of Sirius Radio, Ken Gammage of Directed Electronics, Jim Cavanaugh of Sound in Motion, Mike Hedge of Parrot, Lucette Nicoll of Nicoll Public Relations, Doug Walmisley of Walmisley PR, Jaed Arzadon of Pioneer, Chuck Tannert of *Popular Mechanics* for being a great road trip buddy and friend, Mike Mettler of *Sound & Vision* for being the best (former) boss ever and a solid friend, Hope Edelman of Los Amigos de las Tunas, and Maurice Bourget simply for being Uncle Mo.

Finally, thanks to my agent, Carole McClendon, and the nice folks at Wiley Publishing, Linda Morris, Tiffany Ma, and Melody Layne.

Publisher's Acknowledgments

We're proud of this book; please send us your comments through our online registration form located at www.dummies.com/register/.

Some of the people who helped bring this book to market include the following:

Acquisitions and Editorial

Project Editor: Linda Morris

Acquisitions Editor: Tiffany Ma

Copy Editor: Linda Morris

Technical Editor: Per Schroeder

Editorial Manager: Jodi Jensen

Editorial Assistant: Amanda Foxworth

Sr. Editorial Assistant: Cherie Case

Cartoons: Rich Tennant (www.the5thwave.com)

Composition Services

Project Coordinator: Patrick Redmond

Layout and Graphics: Reuben W. Davis, Alissa D. Ellet, Shane Johnson, Barbara Moore, Christine Williams

Proofreaders: Broccoli Information Management

Indexer: WordCo Indexing Services

Publishing and Editorial for Technology Dummies

    Richard Swadley, Vice President and Executive Group Publisher

    Andy Cummings, Vice President and Publisher

    Mary Bednarek, Executive Acquisitions Director

    Mary C. Corder, Editorial Director

Publishing for Consumer Dummies

    Diane Graves Steele, Vice President and Publisher

    Joyce Pepple, Acquisitions Director

Composition Services

    Gerry Fahey, Vice President of Production Services

    Debbie Stailey, Director of Composition Services

Contents at a Glance

Table of Contents

Foreword

I've been able to drive some pretty sweet cars over the past two decades, thanks to my former job as a car audio journalist — Ferraris, Lamborghinis, Porsches, Mustangs, Corvettes, you name it. But you want to know a secret? As cool as it was opening it up behind the wheel of all of those slick vehicles, I was more interested in cranking their car stereos.

To me, there's nothing like zipping down the open road in a sweet ride with your favorite tunes at your fingertips, and there's no one better to tell you how to maximize that experience than Doug Newcomb, the author of *Car Audio For Dummies*. Doug and I have logged many hours on the road together, traveling in tandem on numerous road trips, highway adventures, and cross-country caravans. Even now, many of our conversations begin with a most familiar question: "Guess what I listened to in the car today?"

This book will show you how to plan, design, and build a great car stereo from the ground up and enjoy it every time you turn on the ignition. Sure, a lot of people are content with the stock systems that come with their vehicles, and it's true that factory stereos have come a long way since the days of tape decks. But if you simply stick with stock, you're missing out on all of the great aftermarket upgrades available. Can you add better speakers and more bass without breaking your lease or tearing up your car's interior? Absolutely. Is it possible to get sound quality equal to that of the best home stereo systems? Sure it is. What about video, satellite radio, and iPod integration? Yes, yes, and yes. You can do it all, and more.

I can honestly say that I've heard car stereo systems that sound better than some of the most elaborate home theater setups out there (and I now evaluate the latter every day). The first time the mobile audio bug bit me, I spent two years auditioning speakers for my car. I'm not saying you need to go to that extreme, but you owe it to yourself to see what's out there and find out how much fun it can be to put together a great car stereo system. And *Car Audio For Dummies* is the key to helping you achieve sonic nirvana on the road.

There are few things Doug and I love doing more than listening to music in a car. So hop in and join us for the ride, won't you? An endless road of car audio possibilities awaits you inside.

Mike Mettler

Vice President/Editor-In-Chief, *Sound & Vision* magazine and former Editor-in-Chief, *Car Stereo Review*, *Mobile Entertainment*, and *Road & Track's Road Gear*

Introduction

Welcome to *Car Audio For Dummies*! My goal in writing this book is to provide you with all the information you need to build the car audio system of your dreams. Whether you want a car audio system that makes it seem as if your favorite band is performing right on top of your dashboard, one that can keep a carload of passengers entertained with music and movies, or one that lets you bring your entertainment media into the car in any way you choose, this is the place to start. This book covers everything from planning your system, to shopping for the components, getting them installed, how to get the most out of your system, and how to maintain and protect it. Think of it as your personal guide to the exciting world of car audio.

About This Book

Although there are certain steps to follow when putting together a car audio system, there's no one-size-fits-all formula. Some people may want to simply upgrade their stock stereo system with better speakers and an amplifier, or just change out the radio or *head unit*. Others want to chuck all of the stock components and start from scratch. Still others may only want to add mobile video to their cars or Bluetooth hands-free-phone capability. Still others want to add all of the above.

Consequently, this book was written in a manner that allows you to get whatever you want out of your car audio system. As such, it's structured so that you can turn to the section that's most applicable to your situation, or read the entire thing to go from a complete beginner to a very knowledgeable newbie.

How This Book Is Organized

This book is divided into six parts, each focusing on a different aspect of the car audio experience: what you need to know and think about before starting to put together a car audio system; various ways you can go about shopping for and installing car audio components; how to select the best components; things you'll need to complete your system and accessorize it; how to best protect your sound investment (and your ears); and, finally, some quick and helpful tips on getting good sound, getting a good deal, and more.

Although I discuss the basics and what's involved with installation of a car audio system, I won't provide step-by-step instructions. That's beyond the scope of this book. I'm also a strong advocate of professional installation. If you have lots of experience with car audio or you know your way around cars and are handy with tools, you *may* want to go it alone. (But hey, if that's the case, you're probably not reading this book!) But modern cars are so electronically complex that one false move could blow an air bag or disable an ABS braking system—and you'll end up spending more repairing your car than you would have on paying a pro to install your car audio system.

Part 1: Starting with Sound Advice

Somewhere there's probably a graveyard of abandoned car audio equipment that people bought but later had no use for. That's because they didn't have a clear idea of what they wanted and why they wanted it. It makes me think of the old saying, "If you don't know where you're going, any path will take you there." You want to make sure the road to your dream car audio system is not a dead end!

Like any purchase, you have to consider whether the car audio components you buy are worth your hard-earned money, of course. But there's the added complication of whether the stuff you buy will fit in your car. After all, a 15-inch subwoofer looks mighty impressive, but installing it in your vehicle may be impractical or even impossible. There's also the matter of whether it'll work with other car audio components in the system and whether it's compatible with future additions to your system. It also comes down to your budget. And you have to think about whether the features you're paying for are worth the money and whether you really need them or will even use them.

It starts with knowing what you want from your car audio system and knowing what kind of mobile music listener you are. You'll also need to consider what types of media you'll be listening to, whether it's CDs or MP3 — or a combination of the two — for example. Maybe you can simply keep your stock radio and add aftermarket car audio components to get great sound with less money and hassle.

Don't discount the idea of staying with a stock system: They've gotten surprisingly good over the last several years. So I look at staying with a stock system as an option for getting to your car audio goals.

To start with, you also need to know what constitutes good sound. I define sound-quality concepts such as frequency response, imaging, and staging so that you know what to listen for. Plus, I recommended some high-quality recordings that help you establish an audiophile reference.

Part II: Shopping for a Great System

Today there are more places than ever to buy car audio components: car audio specialty shops, *big box* retailers, even some auto-parts stores. And, of course, the Internet offers almost anything you want with the click of a mouse. But there are advantages and disadvantages associated with each route, which I detail in this section. I also cover warranties and returns and the option of going with used equipment.

Unlike most consumer electronics that you simply plug into a wall and patch together with a few cables, a huge part of car audio is installation. For one thing, car audio equipment runs on the 12-volt power supplied by a car's electrical system, and wires have to be snaked throughout the car. There's also the issue of how installing car audio equipment affects your warranty.

One of the biggest choices you'll make is whether to have a professional install your gear or attempt to do it yourself. Regardless of your decision, this book tells you where to go and the right questions to ask to get the job accomplished.

Part III: Selecting the Best Components

Selecting your car audio components and installing them is both the most exciting and the most difficult aspect of the car audio experience. It doesn't help that there are hundreds of options to choose from, and every component in a system — from the head unit to the amplifiers to the speakers — has its own unique set of features. But fear not: I break it down so you can make effective and informed choices, and I give you insight on what it takes to get your components properly installed.

Part IV: Tying It All Together

Individual car audio components have to be connected, and different wires in a system do different things. I take the mystery out of car audio cabling and also help you decide whether you need audio *jewelry* or if regular wiring will do. I'll explain why you may — or may not — need power-management accessories such as capacitors, back-up batteries, and high-power alternators. I also cover the importance of other accessories, such as sound-deadening material, and I touch on must-have DIY tools. Finally, I teach you how to tune your system so that you can get the most out of it, and how to keep annoying noise from getting between you and your tunes.

Part V: Protecting Your System and Yourself

If you've done all of the work to plan, shop for, buy, and install a car audio system, you want to make sure you do everything you can to protect it. This includes not only securing your system with an alarm system or some other means, but also making sure that your insurer understands the value of the system should the worst happen: if someone steals it or the car is involved in an accident. In this section, I explain how to enjoy your system but also protect your hearing, as well as protect your life and those around you by not becoming distracted while behind the wheel.

Part VI: The Parts of Ten

In this section, I provide easy-to-remember advice for getting great sound in your car and questions to ask your car audio salesperson or installer when shopping for and installing your system. I also provide steps for you to follow to insure that you'll be enjoying your system for years to come.

Icons Used in This Book

This icon calls attention to pointers to help you in your search for the perfect car audio system.

This icon warns that I'm about to dive into some of the finer points of car audio tech. But don't be intimidated by it: I use easy-to-understand language and terms to break it down.

Although car audio enhances your enjoyment of your car, there's always a potential for harming your car audio components and your ride if things are not done properly and safely. This icon indicates that you should play close heed if you want to avoid any potential problems or mistakes when putting together your car audio system.

This icon signals car audio truisms and important points that you'll want to remember.

Part I

Starting with Sound Advice

The 5th Wave   By Rich Tennant

In This Part . . .

In this part, I help you decide which type of car audio system is best for you based on your musical tastes, your car, your needs, and your budget. I also take a look at the advantages — and drawbacks — of stock car audio systems, as well as why and when it makes sense to keep the factory system or add on to it. I also define sound quality and how to know when you hear it, and point you to recordings to help you reference it.

Chapter 1

Exploring the World of Car Audio

. . . .

. . . .

*I*f you're like me, some of your most treasured memories are listening to an awesome audio system in an automobile. Picture this: It's a beautiful day on a fun road and you're behind the wheel of your car, jamming to your favorite music. Now think of the same situation if you were driving in silence. It's just not the same.

Music makes a good drive even better, a long road trip more fun, a daily commute more bearable. Think of your best times behind the wheel, and chances are there's a soundtrack that goes along with it.

After all, cars and music go together like . . . well, cars and music. Just think of all the great rock, pop, and rap songs that have been written about cars: from The Beach Boys "Little Deuce Coupe" to Prince's "Little Red Corvette" to The Game's "How We Do." In this chapter, I set you on the road to a great car audio system: I cover how to decide what kind of system you really need and want, how to factor in your budget, and how to make the most of what your system already has.

Taking the Car Audio Plunge

For my money, there's no better place to listen to music than in a car. When you're listening at home, the phone always rings or someone tells you to turn it down. Even with headphones, distractions occur and the music is all in your head, so to speak. But the car is like your own private listening room: a mobile sound cocoon that isolates you from the outside world. You can turn it up as loud as you want (as long as you're not disturbing others) and feel the visceral impact that comes from the music pulsing around you.

I've been fortunate enough to hear some ultra high-end home-audio systems and I've been in state-of-the-art recording studios and witnessed some amazing live performances. But none of these live up to the feeling I get while listening to a well-designed car audio system in a cool car on a fun road. Music just seems to sound better when asphalt is flying under your feet!

The best time ever for car audio fans

There's never been a better time to be a mobile music lover. Not only have components such as amplifiers and speakers reached an apex of performance and offer more bang for the buck than ever, but the recent explosion in media options has made the DVD radios that were state-of-the-art a decade ago seem almost antiquated now. The advent of MP3 has freed music from a disc-based format so that now you're able to carry your entire music library on a small portable player such as an iPod. Alternatively, you can load hundreds of songs onto a single disc or even a USB thumb drive. Satellite radio has gained ground against traditional terrestrial radio, while high-definition (HD) radio promises to make AM and FM better and offer more content. Plus, in just a few short years, mobile video has turned "Are we there yet?" to "Are we here already?"

Your roadmap to awesome car tunes

Consider *Car Audio For Dummies* your roadmap to awesome car tunes. You know that there's this wonderful world of car audio out there, but you don't know how to get started planning a sound system, shopping for components, or installing everything, let alone getting the most out of your system, protecting it, and fully enjoying it. In this book, I take you through each step of the process so that you can make informed decisions without wasting time and money and so that you'll ultimately end up with a car audio system that will give you years of listening pleasure.

You've come to the right place

You probably heard someone's car audio system — a friend's, your older sibling's, or maybe one at a car show — and now you want something similar. You used to think your car's system sounded pretty good, but now that you've heard something better, it just doesn't stack up. I've always referred to this as the *ice cream theory*. After you've tasted Ben & Jerry's, for example, you can't go back to the grocery-store brand. It's just not the same.

You know what you want, or at least have a vague idea in mind. You just don't know how or where to get it. The fact that you're reading this book means that you're off to a solid start!

Deciding What Kind of Mobile Music Listener You Are

One of the first things you'll need to determine is how you like your car tunes. Do you like to crank the bass so that people can hear you coming down the road for blocks? Or do you like to hear every subtle nuance of a Mahler symphony? Do you like to be blown away by every note of a great rock-guitar solo and feel the bass drum beating against your chest? Or do you want your system to sound as if Norah Jones and her piano were sitting on your car's hood? Maybe you want your system to do all of these things. The cool things about car audio is that you can have it almost anyway you choose.

 Deciding what kind of music listener you are helps you determine a starting point. Most people have wide-ranging musical tastes, and it is possible to put together a system that bangs out the bass in a rap song and produces the subtle sound of a symphony. Defining those parameters will help you when planning your system.

Besides thinking about what kind of music you mostly listen to, you should also consider how you like to listen to it. Do you mostly drive alone during a daily commute? Or do you want a system that you can crank when you're out driving with your friends? Most people will want a little of both.

 Also think about what type of media options you'll want. Do you keep all your music on an MP3 player, or do you mostly listen to CDs? Are you an FM radio listener or do you like to tune into AM talk radio? Thinking about these things can help you pick out the best components and hopefully avoid some potentially costly mistakes down the road.

In the not-too-distant past, you had just a few choices in music formats: AM, FM, CD, or cassette. But MP3s, the iPod, and satellite radio have changed the way people listen to music in the car. And now it's not uncommon for in-dash radios to sport USB drives or even SD card slots that allow you to play dozens of digital music files on these handy devices. Plus, it's possible to burn as many MP3 and WMA tracks on a single CD as a clunky old CD changer once held on multiple discs. Now, devices such as phones and portable media players (PMPs) that use Bluetooth Advanced Audio Distribution Profile (A2DP) technology to wirelessly wing music to a compatible car radio are starting to become available.

With so many different ways to bring your tunes on the road, it pays to think long and hard about how you'll listen to music in the car. It's a way to hopefully future-proof your car audio system so that you're not shut out from using new technology or having to do expensive upgrades later on.

Finally, creating a car audio system can be an extension of your personality, in much the same way that customizing your car says something about you. After all, if you wanted to be like everyone else, you'd just keep your stock stereo system. Car audio is about creating a system that sounds the way you like it, plays the media that you choose, and looks the way you want it to.

Knowing Your Car, Your Needs, and Your Budget

It's not uncommon to start out with grand expectations when fantasizing about your future car audio system. It's nice to dream, and it's free! But when it's time to come down to reality, you'll need to accurately assess your car, your needs, and your budget to determine what works best for you.

Your car

Although you may want a wall of 18-inch subwoofers that will blow away the boys (and girls) down at the local hang site, if you're driving a Ford Focus, such a scenario is obviously unrealistic. Even if you drive a large SUV, you probably can't fill it up with bulky amplifiers and subwoofers if you use it to transport stuff like kids, groceries, or tools for your work.

You'll also need to consider how long you plan to keep your car. If it's yours for life, you can probably go crazy and turn it into the ultimate sound machine. But if you plan to trade it in or sell it in a few years, keep in mind that prospective buyers may not be as thrilled as you are about the custom car audio system. In fact, contrary to what you may think, a mega sound system sometimes *detracts* from the value of a vehicle.

This is especially true of cars that are traded in at the dealer level. The last thing they want to see is a bunch of non-factory authorized accessories "hanging off of a vehicle," as one auto insider once told me. Consequently, you'll take a big hit on the value. And if you're driving a leased vehicle, you'll want to tread *very* lightly when adding car audio components or any accessories that may alter the car. Otherwise, you could be hit with a penalty at lease end.

Your needs

Have you ever bought something and went with all the bells and whistles and later found out that you don't need them all? Shopping for a car audio system is not much different. You'll want to make sure you get what you need and aren't buying stuff you don't. Although a car's physical space will dictate how much car audio equipment you can install in it, your appetite for the latest and greatest doesn't have such built-in limitations. Consequently, it can sometimes be difficult not to go overboard and overspend on items and features you don't need or will never use.

Think about your listening habits and media preferences as well as your own aesthetics preferences. For example, although it may be cool to buy a head unit with a display that offers 1,000 different colors, is it really worth the extra money you may spend? Or will a subwoofer with lights that blink to the beat really add anything in terms of sound quality — or improve your image on the street? These are questions only you can answer, and you should ask.

Your budget

I like to think of a budget as a self-correcting system. Although anyone can come up with an awesome car audio system on paper — and many enthusiasts both experienced and inexperienced often do — when it comes down to plunking down your cash, writing a check, or whipping out your credit card, the reality of your financial situation takes over.

Therefore, it's essential to take stock of what you can afford and plan accordingly. One of the great things about car audio is you don't have to buy everything at once and you can add on to your system as funds become available. You can start off with a head unit, for example, that powers the factory speakers, and then add aftermarket speakers later on. After that, you can add an amplifier and maybe a subwoofer.

If you do splurge and go for the whole system at once, it's important to allocate your money wisely. For example, you don't want to blow your wad on a super-duper head unit and then skimp on the amplifiers and speakers if you later have to replace them. That's counterproductive and wasteful.

Although there's no magic formula on how to spread a given amount of funds on a car audio system, here's a general guideline on the percentage you should allocate to a given area:

- ✔ Amplifier(s): 40%
- ✔ Speakers: 30%
- ✔ Head unit: 20%
- ✔ Accessories: 10%

Use this as a general guideline when you start planning your component-buying budget, but take it with a few grains of salt. You may, for example, decide to spend more on a high-end head unit and less on amplifiers and speakers.

If you don't plan to install your system yourself — and the fact that you're reading this book should indicate that you probably will not — remember to allot a large percentage of your funds to cover professional installation. Installation generally absorbs up to 40 percent of your overall budget, so adjust your planning accordingly.

I've heard too many stories of over-eager enthusiasts maxing out their credit cards and damaging their credit ratings to get a car audio system they couldn't otherwise afford. As badly as you may want a system for your ride, think long-term and don't do anything stupid. You can add to your system as you have the dough, and many reputable independent car audio shops will work with you if they know you're in it for the long haul and will be back to buy more. They may even cut you a great deal on used or discontinued equipment. So before you go into debt to get that system, think about whether its worth it in the long run.

Choosing between Mild and Wild

For many people, car audio is as much about show as it is about sound. After all, chrome wheels won't make your car go any faster, but they look good, they're fun, and they tell people you care about your car. Nothing wrong with that. After all, people have been pimpin' their rides for years.

If you want a flashy car audio system, go for it. Just keep in mind that there are trade-offs. If your car is a daily driver and you use it to haul people and other things, then going with a flashy system may be impractical. For instance, I once put a *show* system in my 1996 Chevy Impala for a cross-country promotional trip I did for a magazine. It was the first time I installed a huge system in my own personal car after nearly 10 years in the car audio business. Although the interior was kept pretty low-key except for custom door and rear-deck panels for the speakers, the car's trunk was turned into a veritable car audio show-case. It included five amps in a rack in the floor and three 10-inch subwoofers in a bandpass box with a see-through Plexiglas panel under the rear deck. A massive 100-disc CD changer was installed against the driver's side trunk wall, with a bank of capacitors and power-supply accessories on the other. It was all trimmed with custom vinyl-covered wood and Plexiglas panels.

It sounded great and looked awesome. The car was a hit at the shows I attended and my neighbors would bring their friends over just to see it and listen to it. It was covered in magazines several times, and it was cool to have a celebrity car.

But the car didn't handle and accelerate the same due to all that extra weight from the car audio components. About a year or so later, after my first child was born, my wife and I couldn't even fit a baby stroller in the trunk because of all the car audio gear.

The reason I relate this story is to show you both sides of the coin. You can go with a mild system, like the one shown in Figure 1-1. Or, go nuts with a system like that in Figure 1-2. If you want that showy system, by all means, you should have one. But a great-sounding but more discreet system can usually serve the same purpose. Plus, with a showy system you run the risk of attracting the wrong kind of attention: from thieves.

Figure 1-1:
A *mild* system can sound good and leave you with trunk space.

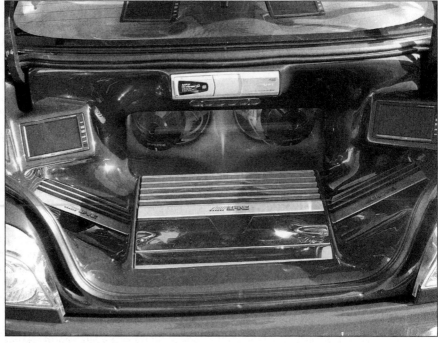

Figure 1-2:
A *wild* system looks great but can leave you with no trunk space.

Upgrade your factory-installed system

If you really want to stay on the mild end of the scale and keep from altering your car too much — as well as protect against theft — you can keep the factory radio and add components such as amplifiers and subwoofers. Inversely, you could always change out your factory radio and keep your factory speakers intact.

I did this in one of my own vehicles, a 1997 VW Eurovan Camper that's a family-mobile. After talking it over with my installer, we decided I could get the sort of performance I needed in the vehicle (after all, my wife mostly drives it, and I can't really crank it up with the kids around) just by swapping out the radio. This also gave me the option to add satellite radio and an auxiliary input that allowed me to easily jack in an iPod. And I could always decide to upgrade the speakers and add an outboard amplifier later.

There are several options for upgrading your factory audio system. You should consider these first if you're primarily looking for better sound. The easiest and least expensive path to better sound is to swap the factory speakers for higher quality aftermarket ones. Many car audio manufacturers offer *drop-in* speakers that are specifically designed to fit factory provisions in a vehicle with a minimal amount of hassle and little to no modification. Often it's just a matter of taking out the factory speakers and *dropping* in new ones. This approach generally offers the most bang for your buck because many stock car audio systems use cheap and poor performing speakers, and even inexpensive aftermarket speakers can offer a dramatic difference in sound quality.

Keep your factory radio

When most people think of a *car stereo,* they think of the thing in the dash with buttons and a display. But such *head units* are just part of the system, although a major part. They generate an audio signal, let you select among various music formats, show what's playing, allow you to crank the volume, and sometimes include some signal processing functions, such as equalization, which tweaks the sound to better suit the car's interior space.

Then they send a signal on to the speakers in a system and sometimes to amplifiers in between to boost the signal. Truth is, many modern stock head units do this quite well, and they are getting harder and harder to extract from the dash. Some are oddly shaped or control other functions of the car, such as climate controls. So it isn't always practical — or even necessary — to replace the radio in some vehicles.

Understanding OEM upgrade options

The increasingly difficult-to-replace head units are why a growing trend in the car audio industry is to leave the factory head unit intact and add components *downstream* in the audio signal path. This is happening for the reasons I mentioned earlier in the chapter, as well as the fact that many people lease their vehicles these days and are reluctant to modify them in any way. Because of this, the aftermarket car audio industry has started to respond with a growing number of components specifically designed to allow upgrading a stock stereo system.

Almost all stock head units have only amplified *high-level* outputs that are designed to drive speakers, not amplifiers, which usually require an un-amplified *low-level* signal. That's why it's typically easier to add speakers to a factory system than amplifiers. Some aftermarket amplifiers do, however, accept both high- and low-level signals, making them ideal for OEM (or Original Equipment Manufacturer — meaning the equipment that came with the vehicle) upgrades. And as with drop-in speakers, adding an amplifier is a surefire way to improve the sound of an anemic stock system.

But it isn't always that easy. More and more stock systems, particularly *premium* systems, also incorporate proprietary signal processing that's designed to work only within the *closed* system. When aftermarket components are added, it can actually make the sound worse because they aren't compatible with the system's signal processing.

But the aftermarket has been performing end-runs around the carmakers for decades. Being the resourceful bunch that they are, car audio manufacturers have responded to being locked out of such systems with products specifically designed to drop a signal from a stock head unit down to line-level *and* filter out any signal processing. Many of these also have an auxiliary input that also allows you to add an iPod or some other audio source to a factory system. If a stock system doesn't use proprietary signal processing, a simple *line-level* output converter will knock a high-level signal from a stock head unit down to *line* or a low-level so that an amplifier can be added.

Regardless, a savvy specialty car audio retailer will be able to help you upgrade your factory system so that you can add almost anything you like to it.

Chapter 2

Considering Stock Systems

*I*f you had told me even a few years ago that a high-end stock system (one that has been originally installed by the automaker) could seriously compete with an equivalent aftermarket system in sound quality and features, I would probably have laughed in your face. But automakers' optional *premium* systems and even some systems available as standard equipment can now rival some aftermarket systems. But make no mistake: Aftermarket systems still offer the ultimate in sound quality, features, and flexibility.

Yet the automakers are quickly closing the gap, particularly with high-end brands such as Mercedes, BMW, Lexus, Infiniti, and Acura. For years, the car companies didn't take audio seriously and their systems were added to vehicles almost as an afterthought. But they've learned, especially in the luxury segment, that it's one way to distinguish a vehicles from its competitors. Regardless of whether large numbers of car buyers shelled out extra bucks for the optional systems, having a *marquee* name on the dash gives the automaker instant audio credibility. Such systems have caught the attention of the general public, however, and the exposure to better sound has raised expectations of how music can sound in a vehicle. And that's a good thing.

In this chapter, I cover the advances that have been made to stock systems in the past few years, and why they can sometimes compare favorably to an aftermarket system. In this chapter, you find out everything you need to know to decide whether sticking with stock is right for you.

What Bose Hath Wrought

The revolution in stock system quality all started in 1983 when GM first began offering premium Bose-branded systems in three of its upscale vehicles. Although this change signaled an improvement over the lackluster stock stereo systems of the day, the early Bose systems weren't the ultimate in sound quality and power. Partly because Bose premium systems represented a threat to the nascent aftermarket car audio industry, they were derided in enthusiast circles as a lowest-common denominator example of quality car audio.

Bose was also the first to use proprietary signal processing and electronics in a stock car audio system, which meant, unlike the standard car stereos of the day, Bose systems couldn't easily be taken out of a vehicle or upgraded. The system architecture was such that they caused headaches for installers.

For example, once while I was covering an installation for a magazine at a car audio shop in Vancouver, Canada in 1989, I witnessed the FM radio in a Cadillac with a Bose system continue to play even after the head unit was taken out of the vehicle! It took installers an hour or so just to locate the *phantom* tuner before they could start in on properly upgrading the vehicle's sound system.

Soon after Bose began to gain traction at car dealers and among consumers, another duo of well-known brands from the home-audio world also entered the stock car audio arena: JBL, in the 1985 Lincoln Continental, and Infinity in the 1986 Dodge Daytona. For years, Bose offered systems in GM vehicles and later branched out into other domestic and import makes. JBL could be found in Ford and later in some import brands (most notably Toyota), and Infinity appeared in Dodge/Chrysler/Plymouth vehicles. These three brands pretty much dominated the U.S. premium stock stereo market into the 1990s.

But it wasn't until Lexus partnered with Mark Levinson, a brand largely known only by high-end home audio enthusiasts (and by then part of Harman International, which also owns JBL and Infinity), that stock car stereo began to seriously compete with the aftermarket in terms of sound quality. And although Mark Levinson wasn't a household name, it's exclusivity immediately set it apart and caught the attention of other luxury carmakers and their discerning customers.

Partly because of the success of the Lexus/Mark Levinson partnership, more high-end home audio brands have since hit the highway, most recently Bang & Olufsen in Audi and B&W in Jaguar. Acura even went to the trouble of creating its own exclusive brand from scratch, ELS Surround, named after and with input from famed music producer Elliot Scheiner. And both BMW and Lincoln have tapped theater-sound specialist THX to create systems for their vehicles.

Aftermarket and Stock: Playing Both Sides of the Fence

In the intervening years, more and more well-known aftermarket brands have been appearing on stock systems. Rockford Fosgate, for example, is now available on some Nissan and Mitsubishi vehicles. (Figure 2-1 shows a Rockford system in a 2007 Mitsubishi Outlander.) Boston Acoustics systems come in some of Dodge and Chrysler's modern-day muscle cars, such as the Charger and 300C. And Alpine has been associated with Jaguar for a number of years, and now the company's products are also available in some Dodge trucks. Even Kicker, long known for their subwoofers in the aftermarket, have cut a deal with Dodge and Chrysler so that subwoofer systems can be added to vehicles as either a factory- or dealer-installed option.

Truth is, many of the major players in the car audio aftermarket have been supplying components to automakers for years, albeit without prominent branding. Clarion, Pioneer, and Alpine all have major OEM divisions that are an important part of each company's overall sales. (OEM stands for *original equipment manufacturer,* which is auto-industry speak for a company that supplies original parts for production cars.) But it's only in the last few years, as aftermarket sales have declined, that many of these manufacturers have blatantly offered *branded* system on vehicles.

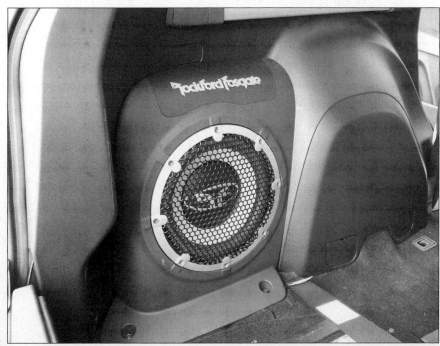

Figure 2-1: A Rockford Fosgate system in a 2007 Mitsubishi Outlander.

Staying with Stock

Just as it would have been unheard of to compare a high-end stock system to a high-end aftermarket setup just a few years ago, I wholeheartedly feel that it's now no longer blasphemous to recommend a stock system as an alternative for some car audio lovers. In the past, stock systems were usually over-priced for the sound and features they offered, whereas the aftermarket provided better sound and better features for less money and maximum flexibility. But the value proposition of stock systems has improved dramatically and the carmakers are closing the gap on features as well.

So (gasp!) it sometimes makes sense to go with a stock system rather than installing an aftermarket one. Ask yourself the following questions when trying decide which route to take:

- ✔ **Do I planning on leasing or buying the vehicle?** If it's a leased vehicle, modifying it could cost you big time at the end of your lease, but if you're buying it you can pretty much do what you want.

- ✔ **How long do I plan to keep the vehicle?** If you plan to sell it within a couple of years, having an extensive aftermarket system could cost you, because it could detract from the resale value.

- ✔ **What features are most important to me?** If you value stereo controls on the steering wheel over sound quality, a stock system may be for you.

- ✔ **Do I want to take the time to shop for and have an aftermarket system installed?** Some people don't want the hassle of shopping for a system or don't want to wait to get it installed, so going with a stock system is instant gratification.

- ✔ **Do I want to possibly permanently alter my car?** Although an aftermarket system can be installed without permanently altering the car, with a stock system you don't take that chance at all.

- ✔ **Do I want to pay for the system all at once or have it spread out over the life of the loan or lease on the car?** One convenience of a premium stock system is that the payments can be spread out over the terms of the loan or lease, whereas with an aftermarket system you usually have to pay for it all at once.

If you're only looking for good sound and don't need every format and feature under the sun, a stock system could make sense for you. On the other hand, if you want something unique and customizing your ride is one of your main motivations, don't check off the premium audio option when you buy the car. Basically, if you don't want the hassle of bringing your vehicle to a car audio shop, picking out components, waiting for the installation to be completed — and you prefer to have the cost of the system built into your monthly car payments — you're a good candidate for a stock system.

Stock mobile video systems

Carmakers have also gotten into the mobile video business as frazzled parents seek ways to keep their kids entertained on long trips. Many car companies offer rear-seat entertainment systems that consists of either an overhead console with a video screen and a built-in DVD player, separate screens in the back of each rear-seat headrests tied to a DVD player elsewhere in the vehicle, or even a screen that flips out of the back of the center console in some sedans. Like aftermarket video systems, these typically come with wireless headphones so that the kiddies can watch cartoons in the back seat while adults listen to car tunes up front.

As with audio systems, the aftermarket can usually beat the OEMs on price, features, and flexibility in the video category. So it's usually better to skip the car dealer's option and buy a video system from the aftermarket. Like aftermarket systems, many stock mobile-video setups have auxiliary inputs that allow Junior to plug in a video game. The fact that mom and dad can roll the cost of the system into their monthly payments is also an advantage for the OEMs.

Stock Systems: Getting Better All the Time

I've been listening to and writing about a lot more stock systems lately, and I've been consistently impressed with their ever-increasing quality. Even the non-premium systems have improved. Another traditional weakness of stock systems is that they're often slow to adopt new technology because the auto industry is tied to multi-year product planning cycles. For this reason, the aftermarket has always been able to adopt new technology much more quickly than the auto industry, but car companies have closed that gap as well.

It took automakers years, for example, to offer iPod integration or even add simple auxiliary inputs so that a portable media player could be jacked into a stock audio system. But Bluetooth capability for hands-free mobile phone use in a vehicle began to appear from the factory even before aftermarket car audio manufacturers began to offer the feature.

As carmakers get more savvy about what consumers want — and align with technology companies the way Ford recently partnered with Microsoft for the Sync system — expect to see stock audio systems offering more technology that consumers are seeking. Although all of this doesn't bode well for the car audio aftermarket, it is better overall for the average consumer.

Chapter 3

Knowing What Sounds Good

You've probably heard a car audio system and was blown away by how great the music sounded — the bass was forceful but tight, the guitars sounded lifelike, and you could hear every nuance of the singer's performance. The bottom line is you noticed a dramatic difference in the sound quality of that system and others you may have heard, and you want to recreate something like it in your own system. But how do you get it if you don't even know what *it* is? In this chapter, I talk about what *good sound* means. After all, you can't get a great system until you know what *great* is, right?

Understanding What Constitutes Good Sound

Great sound is one of those indescribable traits that, like great art or beauty, is in the eye (or in this case, the ear) of the beholder. Yet there are certain qualities that can be indisputably attributed to a great sounding system: clarity, dynamic range, frequency response, and tonal balance. (Don't worry if you don't know what these terms mean — I explain them in the upcoming sections.) Some attributes, such as frequency response, can be measured objectively (by instruments) as well as evaluated subjectively (by ear), whereas others, such as dynamic range and tonal balance, are purely subjective. Sound quality is also very personal: What sounds great to you may sound horrible to someone else.

It's important to design and build your system to suit *your* tastes. After all, it's your car and your money. So if you want a system that's bass heavy, so be it. Or if you want a system with screaming highs, that's cool too. (Just don't ask me to listen to it!) And although you should always build and tune your system to your own sound-quality standards, as with manners, it's better to know what's proper — or, in this case, what proper sound quality is — before you deviate from it.

I've often been asked why I've never competed in *sound-off* competitions, in which car audio enthusiasts go head-to-head to determine who has the best system. (Sound-offs, also sometimes called *crank it up* competitions, can also include SPL, or sound-pressure-level competitions, where the loudest system wins.) My glib response was always that I didn't care what other people thought about my car audio system because it was for my enjoyment. That was only half true, however. I do like to get people's opinions on my system if I feel that they can offer some insight and advice. But I always keep in mind that the system is ultimately for my ears and it's my opinion and enjoyment that matters most.

That said, it's also important to listen to *reference* systems to establish a benchmark. (Reference systems are discussed more in the section "Finding a Reference" later in this chapter.) But first you have to know what you're listening for.

Discovering Aspects of Sound Quality

Remember: Audiophiles can go on and on about the finer points of sound quality in the same way that oenophiles can go on and on about the qualities of wine. (Although you'll never hear an audio fan brag that his system is "nutty, with a hint of raspberry.") My intent is not to turn you into an audio snob spouting esoteric terms, but to help you grasp a few key concepts when it comes to evaluating a car audio system's sound.

The four basic food groups of sound quality are

- ✔ Clarity
- ✔ Dynamic range
- ✔ Frequency response
- ✔ Tonal balance

Clarity

Clarity is the ability of a system to produce the original signal as intended, without distortion. Although this is all but impossible except for the best systems, it's an ideal to strive for. Distortion can be caused by numerous things — from a head unit that's not level-matched with an amplifier to an amplifier that's *clipping* or being overdriven and sending a distorted signal to the speakers. And distortion can come from any component in a system.

To get a sense of a system with exceptional clarity, you'll need to listen to a reference system (discussed later in this chapter) and compare it to a system with unexceptional clarity. A good test is to listen to cymbals, which can have a brassy and off-putting sound when distorted. High-pitched female vocals are also difficult to reproduce and can reveal distortion rather easily.

Achieving clarity and therefore avoiding distortion and is all about proper system design and tuning. It's making sure components are of sufficient quality and compatible with one another and that signal levels are well matched between electronics. It also involves using a component as it was intended and not pushing it past its design limits.

Dynamic range

Dynamic range refers to the ability of a system to reproduce loud and soft passages in music with the same level of detail. When you're at a live concert, a singer may wail and then whisper or a drummer may hit a drum head with brute force and then back off a bit. Each extreme is an important part of the performance.

If the performance is recorded and reproduced by an audio system, the loud and soft parts should be delivered with the same detail and accuracy. But often a system tends to suppress soft parts and emphasize loud ones, meaning you lose the subtleties of the performance.

A related concept is *linearity*, which refers to a system's tendency to lose detail when the volume is turned down. It isn't especially difficult for a system to sound great with the volume cranked. But a system has great linearity if it can retain the same detail at a low volume.

Frequency response

Every sound you hear, from the low rumble of thunder to the high-pitch wail of a siren, is caused by a vibrations in the surrounding air that occur at certain frequencies. These vibrations are measured in hertz (Hz), which refers to the number of times per second these vibrations occur.

A good way to grasp this concept is to think of a guitar string. When a low E note (the largest string) is plucked on a guitar with a standard tuning, the lowest possible frequency it can produce is at about 80 Hz. That means that the string (and hence the air around it that produces the sound) vibrates 80 times a second.

Humans can hear frequencies roughly from 20 to 20,000 Hz. Our ability to hear high frequencies drops off with age and hearing damage, and women typically have better high-frequency hearing than men. Low bass frequencies are felt as much as they are heard, and that's why you feel bass from a passing *boom* car audio system sometimes before you hear it.

A car audio system's frequency response represents how much of the audible frequency spectrum it can reproduce. The frequency response of a car audio system can be measured by an instrument known as a real-time analyzer (RTA), which consists of a microphone attached to a processor with a display that has a graph that shows a system's response.

To measure frequency response, *pink noise*, which sounds like static and contains equal energy across the entire frequency range, is played through the system. Then the system is measured with an RTA, which shows the system's frequency response, usually called the frequency response *curve,* on its display. (See Figure 3-1.)

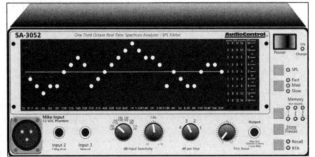

Figure 3-1:
A real-time analyzer displaying a frequency response curve.

Courtesy of AudioControl

The response is described as curved because every system emphasizes or deemphasizes certain frequencies, which is indicated by a rising above or falling below the center line of the frequency response graph. The amount that the response is above or below the line reveals how many decibels (dB), a measure of amplitude or volume, a given frequency range is accentuated or deficient. For example, the frequency response of a system without a separate subwoofer would drop off dramatically below about 75 Hz, whereas a system with too much treble would rise in the high frequencies.

Tonal balance

Ideally, a car audio system would uniformly reproduce the entire audible frequency spectrum from 20 to 20,000 Hz. Although such a *flat* frequency response is theoretically possible, it's practically impossible in the real world because no system — at least while playing music — is perfect. Music is dynamic, meaning that some parts are loud and some are soft, so a system will naturally have *dips* and *peaks* in its frequency response.

Although a system can have these peaks and dips in frequency response, it needs to have good tonal balance — a relatively equal amount of sonic energy across the frequency range — to sound good. Subsequently, system designers and tuners often measure frequency response to gauge which frequencies may need to be *boosted* or *cut* as opposed to trying to achieve a flat frequency response. This can be done with an equalizer, although it's best that the system is designed in such a way that it has good tonal balance to begin with.

Experienced ears can often tell where a good system is lacking in tonal balance just by listening to it, and it's generally easy for most people to discern, for example, when a system lacks response in bass frequencies or if it over-emphasizes treble frequencies. That's why radios have bass and treble controls.

More Advanced Sound Quality Concepts

Although the four sound quality concepts discussed above are the most fundamental, there are a few other SQ attributes that are also important:

- ✔ Timbre
- ✔ Tonal accuracy
- ✔ Staging and imaging

Timbre

Timbre refers to a system's ability to recreate the sound of an instrument as it was originally intended to be heard. An acoustic guitar is usually a good test for this because most people have heard an acoustic guitar. Does the sound have that warm, slightly resonant quality that the instrument is known for, or does it merely sound like a low-resolution reproduction of that signature sound? In other words, does a system reproduce the true timbre of an instrument or a poor imitation of it?

And this doesn't just apply to acoustic instruments. Although some would argue that it's not possible to know the *true* sound of a Roland 808, a popular synthesizer for creating the deep bass sound in many rap recordings, the producer had a sound in mind when he cut the track. How close a system comes to reproducing that sound reflects how accurate it is in timbre.

Tonal accuracy

Tonal accuracy is used to describe how faithful a system is in general to the original recording. It can apply to instruments as well as vocals. The more accurate the system is while playing a good recording, the more you feel as if you are there, listening to a live performance as opposed to a recording.

Tonal accuracy can also apply to the *ambiance* in a recording. Ambiance refers to the *space* in which a recording is made. Most modern recordings are made in a sort of vacuum, with individual instruments recorded separately or, in the case of some rap music, the individual parts are sampled from other recordings. But many older recordings, some modern ones, and almost all live albums capture the environment in which the performance was recorded. In fact, certain recording studios and performance spaces are known and revered for their *sound,* which give a recording or performance a specific ambiance.

Think of timbre and tonal accuracy as the reproduction of how close you get to the actual performance or how the producer intended for it to sound. Whether it's the sound of Miles Davis's trumpet, Jimmy Page's guitar, a Dr. Dre beat, or the ambiance of Carnegie Hall, whether a system can reproduce it the way it went down in a studio or concert hall determines the difference between a good system and a great one.

Staging and imaging

Staging and imaging are related concepts that go back to the heyday of stereo, and therefore don't always apply to modern music. The basic idea is that when you're listening to a stereo recording, the system should recreate the illusion of the stage on which the performance is occurring, and you should be able to pinpoint the sonic *image* of the individual performers and instruments within the stage. (See Figure 3-2.)

Think about the example of a basic rock band that includes a singer, guitarist, bass player, and drummer. In this instance, you should be able to close your eyes and picture the singer at the center of the *stage,* the guitarist to the right, the bass player on the left, and the drummer center and behind the singer. Keep in mind that this is an ideal that sound quality systems should approach if not achieve. With rap and many pop-music recordings, the vocalist will be centered, but the concept of a band playing on a stage doesn't exactly apply.

If you ever go to a sound-off competition or read reviews in car audio magazines, you may hear judges or writers mention something like, "The stage was a bit low and imaging was fuzzy." What this means is that the stage in the car was below, say, dash level and the listener was unable to clearly distinguish the individual performers within the stage. Ideally, the soundstage in a car audio system should be high, wide, and deep, and imaging should be as pin-point as possible. In a vehicle, sonic images are often *pulled* to one or the other side (or both) because speakers are usually mounted in a car's doors.

Speaker placement has a dramatic effect on staging and imaging, and hard-core enthusiasts often go to great lengths to position their speakers for the best possible results. This includes rebuilding door panels or kick panels to better position speakers. Some have even build elaborate mechanisms to mount speakers in or raise them above the dash in order to achieve better staging and imaging.

Finally, no discussion of sound quality would be complete without mention-ing interior acoustics. A car's interior is a huge part of the audio system and plays a dramatic role in a system's response. Beyond the shape and size of a car's interior, it also has reflective surfaces such as glass and absorptive materials such as upholstery. And almost every car interior is different. Therefore, even if you install the exact same components in your Toyota Camry that your friend has in his Chrysler 300C, the systems will sound very different.

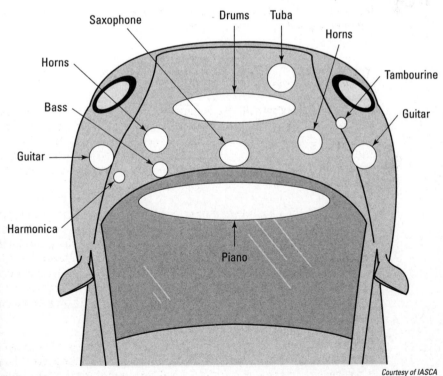

Figure 3-2:
An example
of staging
and imaging
of a car
audio
system.

Courtesy of IASCA

Finding a Reference

Okay, so by now your head is probably spinning with all of this audiophile mumbo-jumbo and you're wondering how you can put it into a practical application. You need a reference. You need to go find the best system possible and listen to it so you know what good sound is and how to apply all of the sound quality concepts discussed previously.

High quality sound systems

One of the most appropriate references is to go to a sound-off near you and ask to listen to some of the best cars there. But you may want to wait until the judging is completed because competitors may be a little reluctant, and a bit nervous, about cranking up their systems until they know how they've done that day. Plus, if you wait until the awards ceremony, you'll know which vehicles are best.

Another way to go about this is to visit a local car audio shop and ask to hear one of their award-winning vehicles. Still another way is to sit in a car with a high-end stock system, such as the Lexus LS 460 with a Mark Levinson Premium system.

To get the best reference possible, visit a high-end home stereo store. They will likely have a demonstration system made up of expensive components. Ask to listen to it with well-recorded music and you'll hear music like you've never heard it before. But be careful: Great sound is a highly addictive pursuit, and you may be tempted to blow tens of thousands of dollars on high-end audio gear!

Test and sound quality CDs

In addition to just listening to the reference system, you also have to make sure to play high-quality recordings on them. A car audio shop or home audio store will likely have some of these on hand. Make note of what they are. It's easy to find reference recordings these days, thanks to the power of the Internet.

The following is a list of several well-known test and sound-quality CDs for evaluation and listening purposes. Some also contain test tones and other such tools that can be used in tuning a system:

✔ ***IASCA Official Sound Quality Reference CD:*** This CD from the International Auto Sound Competition Association, which sanctions sound-off events around the world, contains 42 music tracks for evaluating accuracy, linearity, and timbre, and test tracks for channel and phase verification, noise evaluation, and more (www.iasca.com).

- **Telarc:** This is one of the premier audiophile labels in the US and offers a wide variety of recordings in genres ranging from pop to blues to classical (www.telarc.com).

- **Reference Recordings:** This is an audiophile label that offers jazz and classical recordings (www.referencerecordings.com).

- **Chesky Records:** Another audiophile label, although its classical, jazz, and world-music recordings aren't as stuffy as those of other audiophile labels (www.chesky.com).

Personal favorites

Over the years, I've developed my own stable of recordings that I use to evaluate hundreds of systems. I know these recordings so well that they allow me to instantly pick out deficiencies in a system. (Plus I seem to never get tired of listening to them.) Some are out of print, but you may be able to find used copies online or at your local library:

- ***Bluesiana Triangle* (Windham Hill Jazz):** This is my all-time favorite, a one-off recording featuring pianist/guitarist/vocalist Dr. John, horn player David "Fathead" Newman, and the late great jazz drummer Art Blakey. It features fun jazzy-blues jams that are impeccably recorded with incredible dynamics. I listen for the accuracy with which a system reproduces the timbre of Newman's saxophone, Dr. John's piano, and Blakey's dynamic drums. The nine-minute, mostly instrumental track "Shoo Fly, Don't Bother Me" is also perfect for checking soundstaging: Newman's flute solo should image in the center of the dash and Blakey's cymbal rides should be positioned high within the soundstage. Blakey's bass drum is also good for checking out a subwoofer's dynamic range and a system's tonal balance.

- **Luka Bloom, *Turf* (Reprise):** This Irish singer has a deep, resonant voice that sends the midbass in many systems into distortion, and his high-pitched acoustic guitar makes it easy to pick out problems with high-frequency response and timbre. Bloom's voice should image smack-dab in the middle of the dash and have a tangible quality.

- **Red House Painters, *Ocean Beach* (4AD):** This band's acoustic music is also great for evaluating midbass and treble tonal balance and accuracy as well as dynamic range. If a system can faithfully reproduce the thick midbass barrage in the song "San Geronimo," it passes my test.

- **Joan Armatrading, *What's Inside* (RCA Victor).** This CD kicks off with a deep-bass throb that sends many systems into distortion. Plus, Armatrading's voice ranges from masculine lows to girlish highs, and the deeply layered and well-recorded music allows checking for tonal accuracy, staging and imaging, and dynamic range.

Although you should acquaint yourself with what a good system sounds like, you should ultimately learn to trust your own ears. And the more you listen to high-quality systems, the more you'll become good at picking out deficiencies. If you are going to the trouble of putting together a car audio system, chances are you love music and listen to a lot of it. Ultimately, use what sounds good to you as a guide for creating the sort of system that you'll enjoy for a long time.

Part II
Shopping for a Great System

"He rattled off some nonsense about timbre, linearity, and dynamic range, and before I knew it, I was buying the 'Big-Box-O-Boomin-Bass' package."

In This Part . . .

Shopping for the components for your car audio system can be a fun and yet frustrating experience, and everything has to be installed in your car before you can even begin to enjoy it. In this part, I walk you through the various options available for buying car audio equipment and explain the different routes you can take to get it installed.

Chapter 4

Finding the Right Retail Experience

*S*hopping for your car audio components should be a fun and exciting experience. You've dreamed of putting together your system and scrimped and saved your money to purchase your first round of components. Or maybe you're lucky enough to buy all your gear in one fell swoop. Now it's just a matter of walking into a store or going onto the Internet, picking out your components, getting them installed, and hitting the road.

Well, it's not that easy. But it doesn't have to be difficult either. Finding the right retail experience can make the difference between getting off to a great start or getting frustrated right off the bat in your search for a great car audio system. Every retail route has its advantages and disadvantages and ups and down. It's not that one is better than the other, but one may be better for you for various reasons. And there's no rule stating that you have to do it one way or another. In fact, you may want to blend several different methods to make sure you get the best deal — or at the very least find out what each one is all about and which is best for you. In this chapter, I cover your retail choices, and give you some pointers about how to select one that will meet your needs.

Car Audio Specialty Stores

Specialty shops are to the car audio what gourmet restaurants are to the dining. Just as a fine restaurant will have high-quality ingredients and expert chefs, a car audio specialty store is where you'll find the best equipment and the most skilled installers. It's where innovation usually springs from and sometimes where enthusiasts gather to show off their systems and to see the latest and greatest ones.

Most likely, the first car audio specialty shop was started by someone who was an enthusiast themselves, as opposed to someone who was just out to make a buck. Unlike electronics stores that sell everything from washing machines to computers, a car audio specialty shop, as the name implies, is in business for only one reason: to help consumers create the sound machines of their dreams.

Unfortunately, the number of car audio specialty shops has dwindled quite drastically in recent years. This is not only because factory audio systems have gotten better, but also because there are many more options for getting car audio equipment, such as on the Internet. Also, as with most consumer electronics, prices for head units in particular have fallen in recent years, and the small mom-and-pop car audio shops have had a harder time competing with mass-market retailers and price-slashing Internet e-commerce sites. But chances are you still have a specialty shop or two in your town, and they are still the place to go if you want the best equipment, the best advice, the best service, and the best installation.

Where the experts are

A specialty shop is where you'll find the sort of people who have made car audio their life's work. Hence, it's where you'll find the most knowledgeable and passionate people in the car audio biz. Unlike businesses that sell other electronics or even car parts and accessories, a car audio shop succeeds or fails on the equipment it sells and the service it provides, so they better know what they're doing.

You can look in the Yellow Pages for a list of car audio specialty shops in your area; they're usually listed in the automotive section. But a better way to start your search is to ask a friend or acquaintance who has had a nice system installed for a recommendation. Better yet, attend a local *sound-off* competition or car show and take a look at the cars there. Many times, a show car will have a sign announcing who installed the system, or the shop may have a representative in attendance.

When you visit the shop, check their attitude. Because you'll likely be working closely with the employees of a specialty shop, it's important to make sure it's a good fit. Unfortunately, sometimes shops can have a bit of a snob or clubby appeal. Make sure they take the time to listen to you and answer your questions. If they are inattentive, rude, or condescending, walk out and find another shop. What the shop provides is a service, after all, and if they can't provide that, find one that will. But also don't waste their time with a million questions if you're not serious about doing business there.

Here are some things to look for on your first visit:

- ✔ A friendly, helpful attitude
- ✔ A clean and well-organized appearance
- ✔ A well-stocked product display board
- ✔ A photo album or slideshow of the shop's work
- ✔ Awards or trophies from car shows and sound-off competitions

And here are some questions to ask:

- ✔ Do you have the products I'm interested in currently in stock?
- ✔ Can I see some of your work?
- ✔ Can you give me references to contact other people you've worked with?
- ✔ Have you ever worked on the make, model, and year of car that I own?
- ✔ Do you keep a record of the work you do for insurance purposes or so that it's possible to reference previous work if there's a problem?
- ✔ Do you carry insurance?
- ✔ Do you plan to drive my car?
- ✔ Will you tune the system when the work is completed and is it part of your fee?
- ✔ Will you retune the system in six months when speakers break in and periodically after that?
- ✔ Can I bring my own equipment and have you install it?

And here are some questions they should ask you:

- ✔ What kind of music do you listen to?
- ✔ What kind of car do you drive?
- ✔ How long do you plan to keep the car and is it a leased vehicle?
- ✔ What sort of system do you want?
- ✔ What are your expectations for a system?

You should also bring in some of your favorite music and ask to listen to it on one of the shop's demo vehicles.

What they can offer

The salespeople at a good car audio shop should be very knowledgeable about not only the products they sell, but also brands they don't carry. They should be able to tell you why one brand is better than another, or even why products within a certain brand's line differ from one another. And they should be able to explain in detail the products they sell. They shouldn't bad-mouth brands they don't carry, however.

Many car audio shops carry exclusive and high-end lines of equipment that can't be found in other outlets, as well as more mass merchant brands you'll find elsewhere. With the high-end lines, specialty shops often have exclusive-territory arrangements with manufacturers that stipulate that the same products can't be sold in another store in the vicinity. Manufacturers who supply the top gear also typically make sure the salespeople and the installers are well trained so that the products perform at their best.

A car audio specialty retailer can provide you with personalized, one-on-one service that you can't find anywhere else. They will usually take the time to fully understand you, your needs, and your car. Sometimes they'll take a fledgling enthusiast under their wing and may even give you a break on the price of equipment and installation. Or, they may be willing to give you a package-price discount if you buy lots of equipment and have it installed there.

What it will cost you

As you can probably guess, the expertise and exclusive product offerings of car audio specialty shops also come at a premium price. Although they can often offer the best equipment, installation, and service, they also usually charge more for it. Plus, because they don't buy equipment in huge volumes the way large retailers do and they have higher overhead costs than Internet sites, they either have to charge more or make less profit. But they will also usually work with a customer on price if, for example, they know he is a potential longtime customer.

Specialty shops also have the highest installation-labor rates because they usually have the best installers. Depending on your location, you can expect to pay anywhere from $50 to $110 per hour for installation at a specialty shop. They may also be able to offer different rates for different levels of work. For example, if you just want to replace your speakers, they may have a junior person work on it at a lower hourly labor rate, whereas custom work will be done by a very experienced installer and will cost more.

A specialty shop can also help you put together a custom system just for your car. Want a subwoofer box that fits in the floorboard of the passenger-side front foot well? No problem. And they'll be there when you're ready to upgrade your system.

Finally, they'll be there after the sale and installation to help with any problems or questions. At least you hope so, and they do too. One of the downsides of a specialty shop is, being small and independent, there's no guarantee that they'll survive. As mentioned, specialty shops have become something of a rare breed. One I worked with after recently moving to a different state, for example, went belly up after I'd paid them a few visits. It's a chance you have to take. But you can usually gauge a shop's longevity by how busy they are and based on their reputation.

Big Box Options

In the last few decades, consumer-electronics retailing has become dominated by *big box* stores such as Circuit City and Best Buy. (I could never figure out if they are called that because the stores themselves usually look like big boxes, or if it's because they usually have stacks of boxes around the store.) You probably have one near you if you live in an urban area or even in a good-sized town, and you've probably seen their ads in the paper or on TV. Car audio equipment is also sold through mass merchants like Wal-Mart and Sears as well as some auto-parts stores.

Good prices, but . . .

The biggest advantage of shopping at one of these mass-market retailers or chains is price. Because they buy in such huge quantities, large retailers usually have the best prices. Some even offer to beat the price of any other retailer if you find it cheaper elsewhere.

The big box stores also usually have a wide selection of equipment and brands. In fact, in the past few years, some brands that were formerly found only at specialty retailers, such as Alpine and Rockford Fosgate, are now available in the big box store as manufacturers have had to choose between making a few large profits with specialty stores or a lot of small profits with the big retailers. And the dwindling specialty market has help accelerate this change.

Another advantage of big box stores is that they usually have a finance program that you can sign up for on the spot. So if you have decent credit, instead of paying for your system all at once or even putting it on your credit card, you can spread it out over months. Plus, while some specialty shops also offer financing, most mass merchant retailers also offer interest-free financing for up to a year to sweeten the deal.

But with a big box retailer, you also won't get the personalized and expert service that you can get at a specialty retailer. Chances are the sales clerks won't be steeped in car audio experience the way they are at a specialty shop. The emphasis is usually on moving large amounts of products as opposed to customer service. And while you can rest assured that the big box retailer will be around, the person you work with may not be because there's typically higher turnover in the sales staff. Whereas many employees at a specialty shop live and breath car audio, for employees of a big box store, it's simply a job.

Installation issues

Some big box stores have an installation department, and they've done a great job of improving their service and reputation over the last few years. For example, some Best Buy installers are now certified through the Mobile Electronics Certification Program (MECP), which tests installers' knowledge and skills, and the stores offer a Lifetime Workmanship Warranty. But mass merchants usually have a higher turnover of installers than specialty retailers and they don't attract the most talented installers to start with.

If you are going with a simple to moderate system, a big box store can be a good alternative to a specialty retailer. But they usually can't handle custom work and theirs is more of a one-size-fits-all approach. If you want a truly custom system, a specialty retailer is the only choice.

Buying Online

The Internet has opened up a whole new way to shop for car audio. You can sit at the computer in your underwear while shopping for a subwoofer, for example. (Wearing nothing but your underwear to shop at big box store is generally frowned upon, but you knew that, right?) Plus, it allows you to compare prices at several sites and locations easily, whereas back in the day, you'd have to drive or call all over town to get the same info.

As the Internet has become the place that more people shop, the options for buying car audio products online has also increased. Many of the big box retailers have an online sales department, and a few specialty retailers have also added an e-commerce component to their business. Some manufacturers also have direct online sales. Basically, you can get almost anything you want with a click of a mouse.

Why you can't get everything you want

Okay, you can get *almost* anything you want, but not quite. Some of the high-end car audio companies — such as Focal and Genesis — don't allow their products to be sold online. In fact, they have strict policies against online sales and will not honor warranties if their products are purchased on the Internet. Plus, they want to be able to control as much as possible how their products are installed, because installation can make or (literally) break components and has a profound effect on their performance.

Pimp my browser

If you do decide to shop on the Internet, here are two places to consider:

- ✔ **Crutchfield:** This longtime mail-order company has a sterling reputation, great selection, and excellent customer service. Their Web site (www.crutchfield.com) also has a helpful Outfit My Car section that shows what will fit in your vehicle, and a Crutchfield Advisor section where you can learn about car audio components and concepts.
- ✔ **SoundDomain:** This was one of the first and is still one of the best car audio e-commerce sites (www.sounddomain.com). The site offers a wide selection of car audio equipment and brands (as well as other car performance and cosmetic accessories), installation accessories, a fit guide, pictures of installations, and an active forum where users post questions on everything from car electronics to iPod integration.

Although shopping on the Internet is convenient and sometimes saves money, one downside is you may have to pay for shipping, and you don't get that instant gratification on getting the components the same day you pay for them. Plus, you don't get to see and feel the components you are purchasing. And if you have a problem with a component, you can't just bring it back into a store, the way you can with specialty and mass-merchant retailers. Finally, there's just not the same face-to-face customer-service experience online.

Understanding Warranties and Returns

Like any consumer product, car audio equipment usually comes with a manufacturer's warranty. But unlike most consumer products, car audio equipment has to be installed in a vehicle for it to work. And as mentioned earlier, some manufacturers protect themselves from damage caused by improper installation by extending the warranty only if their products are installed by an authorized dealer. That way they can be assured — and you can too — that the products will perform the way they are intended.

JL Audio, for example, a well-respected manufacturer of subwoofers, speakers, amplifiers and accessories, for years offered only a 90-day warranty for some of its products if installed by a do-it-yourselfer or by an unauthorized dealer, whereas the warranty went up to two years for amps and a year for subs if installed by an authorized dealer or if "the system design and installation integrity are evaluated and approved" by an authorized dealer.

A defective or broken car audio component has to be taken out of the vehicle before it can be replaced or sent back to a manufacturer for repair. A potential bummer is that in some cases the customer has to pay to have the equipment taken out and put back into the car by the dealer. Although some specialty shops and big box stores will eat the labor cost and not bill the customer if the product is still under warranty, others will charge their usual rates to take the component *and* put it back in again. But it's rare for high-quality car audio equipment to break or malfunction, and failure rates are in the five percent range.

Regarding returns, a few manufacturers offer over-the-counter returns through an authorized dealer, meaning the retailer will swap out the component for a new one on the spot. But more commonly, the component will be sent back to the manufacturer or a service center for repair, which could take anywhere from a few days to several weeks. Depending on the retailer you choose, they may decide to replace a busted component with a new one from their stock or wait till the repaired component comes back from the manufacturer.

Here are some important questions to ask regarding warranties and returns:

✔ What is covered under the warranty and what it not?

✔ How long is the warranty?

✔ Will you replace or repair the component?

✔ Will it be an over-the-counter exchange, or will the component have to be sent out?

✔ If it's sent out, how long will I have to wait for the repair, and will you provide me with loaner component while I'm waiting?

✔ Who will do the repairs, and where will the component be sent?

✔ If the component is repaired or replaced, will the warranty be extended?

✔ Who will pay to remove and re-install the component?

Shopping for Used Equipment

One way to save some bucks on your car audio components is to buy used gear. People upgrade components in the car audio system or change cars all the time, and when they do, they usually want to get rid of their used car audio components.

There are some excellent deals out there if you know where to look and what to look for. But you have to carefully consider whether it's worth it versus the money you save. Used equipment usually comes without warranty and the transaction is the epitome of *caveat emptor:* buyer beware. You can never be sure what you're getting.

As a general rule, components without moving parts — amplifiers, equalizers, tuners, and such — are the safest to buy used, although amplifiers often take a lot of abuse and are more prone to failure than the others mentioned. Head units with fold-out screens are also known to malfunction with some regularity. With speakers, the rule of thumb is that the ones with cones that move more frequently — such as tweeters as opposed to subwoofers — get more wear and tear, although subwoofers, like amps, tend to get more mistreatment by people who try to bang out more bass or power than the components are designed to deliver.

Of course, you should check for obvious signs of wear and tear. Even though you can't inspect circuitry inside a component, the outward appearance should give you some indication of whether it was taken care of. Dents, chips, and such should be a red flag. With subwoofers, check for metal shavings attached to the magnet: These could get into the voice coil of the sub and cause past or future damage. With head units, check all of the buttons and knobs to make sure they operate smoothly. Ask the owner for any manuals or accessories that came with the component. Finally, check the serial numbers. If they are missing or scratched off, the unit is likely stolen, and you won't be able to have it repaired.

Compatibility isn't a huge issue with car audio gear, but keep in mind that one manufacturer's head unit often doesn't work with another's CD changer, and sometimes they aren't compatible even it they are made by the same manufacturer. Also make sure to check whether a component needs a proprietary cable or plug.

There are several sources for buying used car audio equipment. The best place to start is among friends and acquaintances because there will naturally be a higher level of trust. Another good place to start is with your local classifieds. That way, you can at least inspect the equipment before you buy it to make sure it's in decent shape. And if you install it and have a problem, you can hopefully return it pretty easily. Regardless, ask the seller to give you a short-term warranty, say, 30 days, so that you have time to get the component installed and make sure it's in good working order.

If you're going to meet someone who has car audio equipment for sale, do it in a public place or bring along a friend. Although it's probably legit, you don't want to take the chance of meeting a stranger while you're carrying lots of cash. Better yet, ask if you can pay with a check.

Pawn shops can also be a good source for used car audio equipment, but have an idea of the value of the gear so you know whether you're getting a good deal. Also ask about the warranty so that you have time to install the component to see if it works the way it's supposed to.

Many car audio specialty stores have used equipment in their stock room they are usually willing to part with. Ask the salesperson if they have anything that will work well in the system you're planning and chances are they'll give you a good deal on it, and maybe even a short warranty.

The Internet is a vast source for used car audio gear and there are several useful sites that have a used car audio gear sections, such as www.sound domain.com and www.automotix.net. Newsgroups such as www.caraudio forum.com and forum.elitecaraudio.com have hundreds of listings for used car audio gear too. You can search for the specific components you want or post a WTB (*Want to Buy*) message for something in particular.

eBay and other online auctions sites are also a great place to shop. But you'll first have to familiarize yourself with the going rate for the equipment you're most interested in. A good way to do this is to check auctions that have already closed to get an idea of what similar equipment sold for. Make sure to find out who pays the shipping charges before the auction ends. Sellers have been know to inflate the shipping fee to squeeze a little more profit out of the deal.

Protect yourself by reading the auction site's safety guidelines. You can also use a third-party escrow service or PayPal to handle transfer of funds. If the seller insists on being paid with a money order or cashier's check, use a U.S. Postal Service mail order because this involves the Postal Service in the deal — and makes it a federal case if the seller commits fraud. Never, ever pay cash when using an online auction site and always check the seller's rating.

With the right research and timing, you could score a killer deal on some great used equipment. Just remember the old saying: If it's too good to be true, it probably is.

Chapter 5

Installing Your System: Going Pro or Going Solo

. . . .

In This Chapter

▶ Considering modern car systems

▶ Understanding your warranty rights

▶ Going with a professional installation

▶ Deciding to go the DIY route

. . . .

*I*f you buy just about any kind of consumer-electronics product, you take it home, plug it in, maybe run a few wires, and you're good to go. Not so with car audio equipment. In fact, you can't even listen to any of the components you bought until you get them installed in your ride. (Unless, that is, you want a car battery in your living room.)

The installation is one of the most important parts of a car audio system. Some would say it's *the* most important part. In fact, an old adage in the car audio world is that the worst gear installed correctly will often sound better than the best gear that's incorrectly installed. Beyond performance, there are also safety issues involved with the installation of car equipment, especially as cars have become more laden with electronic safety gadgets. And by installing additional electronics in your car, you could be taking the chance of voiding your vehicle's warranty. In this chapter, I cover the pros and cons of doing it yourself versus hiring a pro. I also cover everything you need to know to find the right installer, if you decide to go that route, or how to find installation help if you decide to take the plunge and install your own system.

Understanding Modern Car Systems

Today's cars are more complex than ever. Used to be that you could easily slide a radio out of the dash and replace it with a like-sized one. But these days the radio is sometimes embedded in the dash in such a way that it's difficult to take out without doing major surgery.

Removing a radio can also sometimes disable or cause problems with other systems in the car. More and more factory car radios control electronics systems such as climate controls, navigation, and others. And even mid- to low-priced cars feature steering-wheel audio controls that you lose if you replace the radio. Even if the car doesn't have any obvious attachments to the radio, swapping out a radio can still cause problems.

A few years ago, for example, I put a sizable system in a 2001 VW Passat wagon I owned, and I replaced the radio with an aftermarket head unit. The next time I brought my car in for service, the dealership informed me that the shop couldn't diagnose the problem with my car because the diagnostic codes are read through the radio.

So I had to go to my installer to take out the aftermarket head unit and reinstall the stock radio just so I could have the car serviced. Then I had to go back to the stereo shop and have my head unit reinstalled. But this time my installer added a *pigtail* to the radio, which is a piece of wire with the necessary factory connection so I wouldn't have to go through that hassle again.

Modern cars also have much more sensitive and sophisticated electronics onboard than did older models. When I started in the car audio industry in the late 1980s, no one had to worry about blowing an airbag or causing a fault with the ABS braking system. These days, making a mistake when installing your own car audio system can not only be costly but deadly.

Warranty issues

When doing it yourself, you also have warranty and lease issues to consider. Although you can install anything you want on your car, if it's under warranty the dealer may — and often will — try to blame the aftermarket car audio parts for the problem. I've seen it happen with everything from alarm systems to amplifiers. Even if that new subwoofer system you installed, for example, has nothing to do with why your transmission fell out, it will immediately be suspect in the eyes of the service writer at a dealership.

Magnuson-Moss Warranty Act

The good news is that you have the law on your side. The Magnuson-Moss Warranty Act of 1975 was passed to protect consumers from being wrongfully denied warranty coverage by new car dealers for various reasons. Of particular interest to car audio enthusiasts is that, under the act, aftermarket equipment added to your vehicle does not automatically void a vehicle manufacturer's original warranty unless

- ✔ The warranty clearly states that it does
- ✔ It can be proven that the aftermarket add-ons were the direct cause of the problem

Rules and regulations that govern the interpretation and enforcement of the Magnuson-Moss Warranty Act state:

"No warrantor may condition the continued validity of a warranty on the use of only authorized repair service and/or authorized replacement parts for non-warranty service and maintenance."

And: "... a warrantor cannot, as a matter of law, avoid liability under a written warranty where a defect is unrelated to the use by a consumer of unauthorized' articles or service. This does not preclude a warrantor from expressly excluding liability for defects or damages caused by such 'unauthorized' articles or service; nor does it preclude the warrantor from denying liability where the warrantor can demonstrate the defect was so caused."

What this means in plain language is that the car dealer must prove that the car audio equipment you added to your vehicle directly caused the need for repairs before denying warranty coverage. If a dealer is trying to weasel out of servicing your vehicle under warranty because you installed, say, a different head unit, speakers, and added an amp, that's one thing. But if you add a high-output alternator to your engine so that you have enough juice for your mega system in your new Hyundai and it causes the engine to catch on fire, the dealer is probably within his rights not to honor the warranty and drop in a new engine.

Using the earlier example of my VW Passat, a dealer can also refuse to service your car if the aftermarket parts you added prevent it from doing so. And they are within their rights to charge you the extra labor required to perform the service because of the addition of aftermarket parts. For example, they could have charged me to install the radio back in the car so that they could perform the diagnostics.

SEMA and CEA on your side

Besides the Magnuson-Moss Act, you also have the Specialty Equipment Market Association (SEMA) and the Consumer Electronics Association (CEA) to back you up. SEMA is the trade group for the aftermarket auto-parts industry, whereas CEA is the trade group for, you guessed it, the consumer electronics industry. Both lobby Congress on behalf of consumers being able to add car audio equipment to their vehicles. Click on www.sema.org and www.ce.org for more info.

"Lease" is the word

If you leased your car, aftermarket installations get sticky because you signed a piece of paper saying you wouldn't permanently modify the vehicle in any way. But fear not. I've seen some pretty sweet systems installed in leased car in such a way that the vehicle can be returned to its stock condition.

Although you may not be able to install a 10-inch subwoofer in each door, you can probably find a pair of drop-in speakers that fit in without modification. And you can add a prefabricated, amplified sub box to get some decent bass. Some shops will even install a custom system that leaves no trace after the components are taken out, although you'll have to weigh whether going to such an extent is worth it given how long you have the car.

Exploring the Advantages of Going Pro

It's my opinion that professional installation is the way to go for beginners. Heck, these days, I think it's the way to go for all but the hardcore and experienced do-it-yourselfers. I've spent considerable time scrunched underneath dashes swapping out radios and curled up in trunks installing speakers, and even I now leave installation to the pros. (And it's not just because I'm too old to contort my body like that!)

As mentioned earlier in the chapter, modern vehicles are too complex to poke around in if you don't know what you're doing. You could easily end up ruining your car audio components as well as your car. If you drive an older car and aren't concerned with this, you may want to go the DIY route. If you do plan to have your system professionally installed, it will add to your overall budget and cash outlay, of course, but it will probably be worth it in the long run.

Here are some advantages of going pro:

- ✔ The system will be installed more quickly.
- ✔ The installation will likely come with a warranty.
- ✔ Your equipment warranty may be extended.
- ✔ There's less chance you'll void your car's warranty.

A professional installer also has better access to information, such as product updates and technical support from equipment manufacturers. Plus, they have all of the tools to make the job go smoother and faster. Finally, they usually know tricks to make a system sound better and can tweak and tune a system for optimum performance.

Most people have their equipment installed at the same place they buy the equipment, but that's not always the case. Whereas some shops install only what they sell, others charge a standard labor rate to install just about whatever equipment you bring in. Make sure you check first.

Typically, a specialty shop can offer the best installation — and the best installers — whereas big box stores generally handle only the most basic installations, such as installing a new head unit or speakers. So if it's a complex system you're after, go to a specialty store. But if you just want new speakers, that's something a mass merchant's installers can do.

MECP certification

Because cars have gotten so complex, car owners want to be assured that the person installing audio and video equipment has some experience and credentials. And as car audio equipment has gotten more sophisticated, car audio manufacturers want to be assured that their equipment gets installed correctly so that the customer is happy with their purchase.

Because of this, car audio manufacturers and installers got together in the early 1990s to create a way to test and certify installers. The Mobile Electronics Certification Program is administered by the Consumer Electronics Association (CEA), which tests and certifies installers on installation techniques and knowledge.

Certification levels include

- ✔ Basic Installation Technician
- ✔ Advanced Installation Technician
- ✔ Master Installation Technician

Installers are required to pass a written exam and meet experience criteria, and they are recertified every two to four years depending on their level.

If you plan to have your system professionally installed, one of the first things you should look for in a car audio shop is the MECP logo, as shown in Figure 5-1.

Figure 5-1:
The MECP
logo.

But there are other things you should look for, including

- ✔ A clean and well-equipped showroom and installation area
- ✔ Examples of the shop's work, either in the form of a photo album or computer slideshow
- ✔ Letters of recommendation from previous customers that may be framed and hung on the wall

✔ Plaques or stickers showing that the shop is an authorized dealer for the brands it carries

✔ Business license or tax certificates

✔ A demo vehicle that lets you see the shop's work and listen to one of its systems

Questions to ask

Remember that you are interviewing the shop and its personnel to determine whether you want to work with them and give them your money. Here are some of the questions you'll want to ask:

✔ Are your installers MECP certified?

✔ What kind of training do your installers have, and how long have they worked here and as an installer?

✔ Can you provide references or names of previous customers I can call?

✔ Are you insured so that I'm covered if something happens to my vehicle?

✔ Will you be driving my vehicle and, if so, why?

✔ What are your installation rates?

✔ Do you provide a warranty on your installations? If so, for how long?

✔ Do you guarantee a noise-free installation, so that it doesn't create alternator *whine* or other types of interference?

✔ What's your service policy if a component breaks?

✔ Will you give my factory stereo or my old aftermarket car audio components back to me when you're done?

✔ Do you use wiring harness adapters so that I can re-install my factory stereo if I choose? And how much modification will you do to my car?

✔ Do you make wire connections using T taps, solder, or crimp connectors? (Avoid an installer that uses T taps: They're unsafe because they don't provide a secure connection. They can loosen and therefore cause a short circuit and possibly damage your components and vehicle. Crimps are okay if done properly, but solder is the best method.)

✔ How do you determine what factory wires to tap into? A good shop uses a computer program to tell which wires to use for an install, and they'll verify the wires using a digital meter.

If an salesperson or installer seems evasive or even arrogant, you should head for the exit right away. Even if a shop does great work but treats you poorly from the beginning, the relationship will only go downhill from there. They should be there to help you, or they may not be in business long, which is another reason to go elsewhere.

On the other hand, if they take the time to answer your questions thoroughly and courteously, you've probably found the right shop. You should also ask to see the installation bay. If it looks neat and organized, that's a good sign. And if they are working on nice cars, that's another positive sign.

Installing It Yourself

If I haven't intimidated you yet and you still want to install your system yourself, there are some things you need to know. Although car stereo installation started out as a DIY hobby, cars have changed significantly since the late 1970s when I installed my first radio and rear-deck speakers in a 1968 Ford Fairlane.

Know your car and your limitations

If you're driving a 1971 Chevelle, you probably won't encounter too many problems: Its electrical system is pretty simple and straightforward. But if your car is a 2006 Honda Civic, you'll want to proceed cautiously because the car will have some rather sophisticated electronics. Cars today have onboard computers, for example, and frying one while installing a head unit can cause big headaches.

As I mentioned earlier, a vehicle manufacturer can't void your warranty simply because you installed aftermarket car audio gear unless it can prove that the equipment led to the malfunction for which you're claiming warranty coverage. But even if your car is not still under warranty, you still want to tread carefully.

You'll have to pull off panels to install components and runs wires, and professional installers have special tools just for this purpose. If you try a DIY install, keep in mind that you risk damaging your vehicle or at the very least not being able to put it back together the way it was before. If you're willing to take that chance with your car, you can save a little money and learn something too.

Besides knowing your car, you should also know yourself and your limitations before starting on a DIY install. Do you love to get your hands dirty and find out how things work? Or do you get easily frustrated and tend to focus on the end result instead of the process? Do you like challenges and learning by trial and error? Or do you prefer to just pay someone else to do the hard work so you can enjoy the benefits?

There's certainly no shame in having someone else do your dirty work when it comes to car audio. I stopped doing my own install years ago when I determined that others can do it much faster and better than I can. It's important to really be honest with yourself before installing your own car audio system.

If you do decide to take it on, here are two DIY projects that shouldn't present too much difficulty, could save you a few bucks, and will help you get your feet wet:

- ✔ **Drop-in speakers:** Ideally, you should be able to just swap out the factory speakers for aftermarket ones. The trick may be in getting to the speakers, because you may have to remove the door panel. In older cars, removing a speaker grille is easier. Then it's just a matter of unscrewing and disconnecting the factory speaker and doing the opposite with the new one.

- ✔ **Single-DIN head unit swap:** If you're doing a straightforward install of a new single-DIN head unit (one that's the standard size, 7" wide by 7" deep by 2" high) and the radio isn't tied into other systems in the car, the degree of difficulty isn't too high. It's usually a matter of removing the radio or removing a dash panel or two to get at the radio for removal. An installation kit, also known as a *fit kit* to keep the radio snug in the dash, may be needed. You should use a vehicle-specific wiring harness adaptor (available from a car stereo store or online) to make it easier to connect the radio's wiring to factory wiring.

Manufacturers' warranties

All manufacturers offer a warranty on their products, although some significantly shorten it if the products are not installed by an authorized dealer. If you buy low-end to *mid-fi* equipment, this may not be a big deal because the warranty on these products is often the same no matter who installs them. But if you invest in high-end gear, the stakes are much higher because the manufacturer will only warranty the product for a very short time, if at all. In that case, it usually pays to pay for professional installation. In any case, make sure to check the warranty on the products you buy, and read the fine print!

Where to Get Help

If you do decide to go it alone, you're not *really* alone. There are people and places you can turn to for help with your DIY installation questions. Chances are you didn't become interested in car audio in a vacuum and have friends who are also into the hobby. Few things are as fun and satisfying as hanging out with your buddies and working on your cars. Find someone who will mentor you or at least answer your questions. Sometimes the shop you bought the equipment from will offer some help or advice. A professional installer may be willing to help you out if you get into a jam.

The 'Net effect on DIY

The Internet has changed everything, of course. Now information is just around the next Web page and it's usually free. Car audio enthusiasts are typically a helpful bunch and don't mind sharing their knowledge — and opinions — with the world. Just remember: Advice is usually worth what you pay for it.

Before the Internet, the only way to get DIY help was to hook up with a friend or buy a book or magazine. But now the Internet is crawling with help on Web sites and forums. Some even have detailed installation instructions and diagrams. Some to check out include

- ✔ Crutchfield, www.crutchfield.com
- ✔ CarStereo.com, www.carstereo.com
- ✔ Basic Car Audio Electronics, www.bcae1.com
- ✔ Car Audio Help, www.caraudiohelp.com

Several online forums also provide installation advice and tips. Some of the best and most active ones include

- ✔ rec.audio car, www.mobileaudio.com
- ✔ CarAudioForum.com, www.caraudioforum.com
- ✔ SoundDomain, www.sounddomain.com
- ✔ Termpro, www.termpro.com

Of course, one of the things that makes the Internet such a great place to get info is its collaborative nature. Anyone anywhere in the world can contribute info, and they usually do. But that's also one of the downsides of the Internet: The information isn't always useful. At online forums, you'll get tons of opinions and advice, for what it's worth. If you follow the discussions, you can learn a lot and, after a while, generally be able to separate the wheat from the chaff.

Magazines

Finally, some car audio magazines offer DIY help, but these are generally of the high-end variety. *Car Audio and Electronics* magazine, for example, taps some of the best installers in the business to do step-by-step installation stories. But these tend to be focused on advanced projects such as building custom door panels or subwoofer boxes. Still, it's good to see what sort of work goes into a project if you are thinking about going the DIY route.

Part III
Selecting the Best Components

The 5th Wave   By Rich Tennant

Harriet's First Gig

"C'mon! Allegro vivace! Allegro vivace! We're selling ice cream not coffins!"

In This Part . . .

A car audio system is made up of individual components that together equal more than the sum of their total, and each piece is critical to overall performance. These days, you have more products than ever to choose from, but that also means that buying the best components can be challenging. In this section, I detail all your options so that you can make informed decisions when shopping for components.

Chapter 6

Starting with the Head

*S*ay the term *car stereo* and most people think of the thing in your dash with knobs and lights that you stick a disc into. But the in-dash part of a car audio system is only a small, if important, part of the whole. Also known as a car radio or a *head unit* in car audio industry parlance (because it's at the head of a system), the head unit is the most visible part of a system and one of the only components you regularly interact with. Because of this, it has to be easy and safe to use when you're motoring down the highway.

The head unit is also the only part of a system that generates an audio signal and it's a conduit for various media options. Only a few years ago, you had just a few choices when it came to media: AM and FM radio, CD, cassette, and maybe DVD. But in the last few years, there's been a huge proliferation of new mobile-media options that allows you to bring music and video into the car in myriad ways.

MP3 and other digital music file formats forever changed how people store music, whereas the iPod phenomenon revolutionized the way people access and carry it. Now you can burn hundreds of files onto a CD or carry your entire music collection on a portable media player (PMP) like the iPod. And you can also store dozens of digital music files on SD cards or a USB drive, and now even on your mobile phone. That doesn't even include the latest over-the-air music options, such as satellite and HD radio.

In this chapter, I look at all the different head unit options that are available to help you decide which is best. So whether you're a CD collector, MP3 maven, iPod aficionado or some combination thereof, you'll get the head that's right for you.

Choosing CD or DVD

The majority of car audio head units currently available are either AM/FM/CD or AM/FM/DVD receivers, with CD-based heads outnumbering DVD-based heads by a considerable margin. Which you choose will largely depend on your music collection as well as your budget because DVD receivers are a bit more expensive. But you should also look beyond the disc and consider the other media options a head unit will provide.

If you mostly listen to CDs, a CD receiver is the obvious — and least expensive — choice. But because even budget-priced CD receivers now come with the option to add external sources, such as an iPod, satellite radio, or USB drive, you don't necessarily have to be restricted to CD-based entertainment. And with CD becoming somewhat of a dinosaur format, even if you do buy a CD receiver, you'll want to give yourself other media options. (More on CD obsolescence later in this chapter.) If you anticipate that your system will be part of a larger car audio/video system, a DVD receiver is the obvious choice.

After DVD was introduced in 1997, it quickly became the most successful consumer electronics product ever, as people abandoned their clunky old VCRs for DVD players and the more robust but familiar-looking DVD. The format also kick-started the mobile video boom of the last few years because it finally created a convenient way to bring video into a vehicle.

If you do plan to make video a part of your system, you'll definitely want to consider a DVD receiver. Although it may be more expensive, a DVD player adds features not found on a CD-based head unit beyond video capabilities. It can store many more music files, such as MP3, for example. It also offers the option to play DVD music discs, which have a higher resolution (hence better sound) than standard CDs. Finally, DVDs offer multi-channel surround-sound formats that let you hear your music in a whole new way.

But the main reason to go with a DVD-based head is for its video capabilities. Many DVD heads have what's known as *dual-zone* capability. This means that a DVD head unit can send a video signal to, say, screens in the rear of the vehicle and allow passengers to listen to the audio portion of a video on wireless headphones. And the DVD head can simultaneously be playing another non-disc source, such as radio or an iPod, over the speakers for front-seat occupants. In this way, the car has two *zones* of entertainment, and two sets of happy people. This works especially well for families, so that the kids can be kept entertained in the back seat while the parents listen to music up front.

Some DVD players also offer DVD-Audio playback. This high-resolution, multi-channel format (not to be confused with lower-resolution DVD music discs) offers the ultimate in sound quality and has bonus features like those found on DVD videos. Unfortunately, this format never really caught on with the public and record companies never fully supported it either.

Before PMPs like the iPod took off, it looked like DVD would dominate the audio/video world, and this has pretty much been the case in home entertainment, where CD players are about as popular as VCRs. But CD has hung on as a significant if slowly dying force in the car audio world, mainly because CD-based heads are cheaper than DVD head units. But if you can afford to go with DVD instead of CD, the extra features and flexibility are worth it.

How the iPod Changed Everything

When DVD first started to take off in the late 1990s, I spoke with an engineer in the recording industry who predicted that DVD would be the last disc-based music format for consumers. This was in the early days of MP3 and a couple of years before the iPod was introduced in 2001. Now, that person's prescient prediction has pretty much come to pass. I just hope he bought Apple stock!

No one could have predicted how Apple's iPod would change the way people store, listen to, and carry music. Although MP3-based PMPs had already been around for a few years, with its elegant yet simple design, intuitive interface, and Apple's straightforward iTunes software, the iPod became a phenomenally popular product the likes of which the consumer electronics industry has never seen.

Now we think nothing of carrying our entire music collection on a device that conveniently fits in a pocket or purse, instantly allowing access to tunes anywhere and anytime. Where normally you'd have to carry dozens of clunky, easily damaged, and space-consuming discs on a long road trip, now you can bring enough music for the journey (and then some) easily on your iPod.

Ever since the iPod hit critical mass, people have demanded a way to bring it on the road, and car audio companies and automakers were all caught behind the curve. The first aftermarket and OEM iPod solutions didn't appear until early 2003. Since then, a whole cottage industry has sprung up to provide iPod integration to vehicles, and now the iPod is only one way to bring massive amounts of music into the car.

Although CD is still the most widely available format among car audio head units, its days are undoubtedly numbered. CD sales are in a steep decline as people are abandoning the disc in droves for music formats that are more convenient and less costly.

DVD is still the preferred medium for movies, but for how long? With movies now available on iTunes and through other online services and with the ability to watch them on non-disc-based players, DVD's dominance is being challenged and the format could go the way of the CD soon.

Disc-less digital music files are undoubtedly the wave of the future and CDs and DVDs will one day be regarded with the same sort of nostalgia that the vinyl LP is viewed today. But this is also a boon for the car audio enthusiast: Not having to deal with bulky discs that are easily damaged will make the mobile music experience more convenient and potentially less costly.

Music files go mobile

MP3 is the computer music-file format that let the digital genie out of the bottle by essentially freeing digital music from the disc. Instead of record companies deciding what music you could have on a CD, now people who already owned the music on CD — and some who didn't and obtained files on peer-to-peer file-sharing sites like Napster — could rip MP3 files onto their computer's hard drive and then burn them in any combination they chose onto recordable CDs. This also allowed storing hundred of songs on a single recordable CD, a technology that went hand in hand with MP3s. It took the concept of the mix tape into the digital age.

MP3, which is short for MPEG-1 Audio Layer 3, was first coined as a file exten-sion (.mp3) for music files in the early days of the Internet and soon became the gold standard for moving music from CD to the computer. MP3 is a *lossy* compression algorithm that reduces the amount of data needed to represent an audio recording, yet still sounds like a faithful reproduction of the original uncompressed sound to most people's ears. The compression removes parts of the sound in a recording that cannot be heard by most listeners and, as a result, much less space is needed to store an equivalent-sized music file.

Space versus sound

The downside to MP3 is that there's an inherent trade-off between file size and sound quality. When creating an MP3 file (while ripping files from a CD, for example), the user can typically select a bit rate that specifies how many kilobits the file may use per second of audio. The lower the bit rate, the smaller the file size. A small file size means that more files can fit on a hard drive or disc, but the sound quality will be lower. Conversely, the higher the bit rate, the higher the quality, but the larger the file size and the fewer songs you can fit on a hard disk or CD. So the choice comes down to storing tons of tracks at lower sound quality on a CD, for example, or a lower number of tracks at a higher sound quality. A 700MB CD should hold about 150 four-minute MP3 songs ripped at the nominal rate of 128 kbps.

When converting a file to an MP3, bit rate can be varied from 32 to 320 kilobits. *CD quality* MP3s are typically converted at 128 kilobits per second, although more demanding music recordings can require encoding at 192 kilobits per second or higher. Most MP3 encoders, however, simply use one bit rate for an entire file to make the process easier and faster.

You can also create files in which the bit rate changes throughout, and these are known as variable bit rate (VBR) files. In any piece of music, some parts will be easier to compress (such as quiet passages or silence), whereas others will be more difficult (complex musical passages). The overall sound quality of the file can be increased by using a lower bit rate for the less complicated parts and a higher rate for the more demanding ones.

With some MP3 encoders, the user can specify a given quality and the encoder will vary the bit rate accordingly. This way, users can select one value when encoding their music without having to hassle with determining the correct settings for their entire music collection and selecting one rate for everything.

Doing Windows

In 1999, Microsoft introduced the WMA (Windows Media Audio) digital-file format to compete with MP3. WMA files are encoded in much the same way as MP3s, but Microsoft claims WMA has a higher sound quality than MP3 and other lossy file compression formats. (The claim has been both refuted and substantiated in numerous *double blind* listening tests.) Regardless, all you need to know is that WMA, along with MP3, is a file format supported by most car audio manufacturers. Also, keep in mind that many people use the term *MP3* generically to describe all types of digital music format.

The reason you need to know all of this is that many CD and DVD receivers in both the aftermarket and in stock systems now supports MP3 and WMA playback. This means you can potentially burn hundreds of music files onto a CD or DVD and then take it into your car.

Many MP3-capable heads also support ID3 tag info. ID3 is metadata (information about a particular file) attached to a music file. The metadata enables the radio's display to show artist and track info, for example, when a music file is playing.

The disc-less drive

It would have been difficult to imagine a car audio head unit without a disc drive only a few years ago, but now it's looking like the future. Alpine and Clarion concurrently introduced the first disc-less head units at the Consumer Electronics Show in January 2007.

Alpine was the first car audio manufacturer to add iPod integration to an aftermarket head unit, so it's not surprising that the forward-thinking company would be the first to offer a radio specifically designed to accommodate the iPod. An iPod connects to the iDA-X001 (see Figure 6-1) with a supplied USB cable for access speed equal to that of the player itself. The head unit's controls and displays mimic that of the iPod, allowing access to files by playlist, artist, album, song, genre, and more. The iDA-X001 also has a 2.2-inch high-resolution screen that makes text and menus easy to read at a glance and it also displays full-color album art. And 24-bit digital-to-analog converters and Alpine's proprietary MediaXpander processing enhance the sound of compressed-audio formats.

Figure 6-1:
Alpine's iDA-X001 head unit doesn't have a disc drive and is designed specifically to work with Apple's iPod.

Courtesy of Alpine Electronics

Clarion's FB275BT head unit was another disc-less model introduced at the 2007 Consumer Electronics Show. Instead, it has a slot for an SD card behind its fold-down faceplate. ID3 tag information such as artist and song title is displayed on the FB275BT's color display.

With the CD going the way of the cassette in the car, look for more manufacturers to introduce head units without a disc mechanism. This is not only of benefit to music lovers in the MP3 era, but it also means that in-dash head units will have fewer moving parts and are therefore potentially less likely to break.

Chapter 7

Carrying All Your Tunes

*B*ringing lots of tunes on the road with a CD changer and lots of bulky discs is now *sooo* twentieth century. In the late 1990s, I installed a 100-disc CD changer in the trunk of one of my cars for a cross-country trip. At the time, it was the only way to bring a ton of tunes along. But I knew something was amiss when it took an hour or so just to load up the thing. I've since taken the mega-changer out, and now I can carry 10 times as many tunes on my iPod, which is one-tenth of the size.

MP3 players such as the iPod have irreversibly changed the way people carry music into the car. The advent of the MP3 has especially been a boon to mobile-music lovers because it's now easy to take thousands of digital tunes on the road. Although disc-based head units still dominate, most now offer some way to let users have access to their large libraries of digital music files.

Today more than ever, the way you carry your music files on the road — be it with an MP3 player like the iPod, burned onto a disc, loaded on a USB drive or SD card, or even on a hard-disk drive — will determine what sort of car audio head unit or system you choose. You can even have several different portals for access to your tunes within a single car audio system. These days, the digital-music options are only limited by your imagination and budget.

In this chapter, I explore ways in which you can bring your entire music collection on the road . . . without installing a dozen 100-disc CD changers in your ride. Because Apple's iPod dominates the MP3 player market, most of the ways to integrate an MP3 player into a car stereo are iPod-specific. But we'll also look at other MP3-friendly portals, such as USB drives and hard-disc drives.

Invasion of the iPod

Apple's iPod wasn't the first MP3 player. Others were around several years before it. And it wasn't the least expensive by a long shot. But the iPod was the MP3 player that captured millions of music lovers' hearts and minds, music collections, and pocketbooks. The iPod quickly became a status symbol as much as a phenomenally popular product, and, in the process, it changed the way people buy, listen to, and store music.

The iPod also changed the way people access music in the car. In just a period of a few years, it's made the CD changer virtually obsolete. Why bring a half dozen discs or more along for the ride when you can carry your entire music collection in your pocket? It didn't take long for the consumer-electronics industry, the car audio aftermarket in particular, and even some carmakers, to respond to the growing number of iPod owners who wanted to take their iTunes on the road.

Today, there's a billion-dollar industry based just around iPod accessories, and car accessories form a large chunk of this lucrative market. iPod integration has also become a driving force in the aftermarket car audio industry because the desire to use an iPod in the car has driven more consumers into car audio specialty shops and other car audio outlets.

Just as CD changer controls were popular features on car audio head units in the 1990s, now many heads have an auxiliary input for an iPod or even full iPod integration. Carmakers have also gotten into the act as consumer demand for pimpin' a ride with an iPod has increased.

Today, you can access an iPod from behind the wheel in a wide variety of ways:

- ✔ FM modulators that send a signal to a car's FM radio
- ✔ Aftermarket head units that have direct iPod input and controls
- ✔ Aftermarket adaptors that can add iPod integration to factory stereos
- ✔ Auxiliary (aux) jacks in aftermarket or stock stereo systems
- ✔ Aftermarket amplifiers and processors with aux inputs
- ✔ Kits available from car dealers that integrate an iPod with a factory stereo and the car's controls

FM modulators

FM modulators have been used for years to add a CD changer to a factory stereo system, or even in aftermarket systems where a direct-connection between the head unit and the changer isn't available. The concept is simple:

The audio signal from the CD changer is fed into an FM modulator, which converts it to an FM signal. The head unit's antenna lead is fed into the FM modulator and a separate antenna lead from the FM modulator — which now carries the AM and FM signals, along with that of the converted signal from the CD changer — is plugged into the head unit.

The FM modulator lets you choose an FM frequency on which to tune in the CD changer, which is usually in the 88.1 to 89.5 range. When the car's FM receiver tunes to that frequency, which is hopefully empty, it picks up the signal from the FM modulator the way it would a regular radio station.

Wireless FM modulators that don't have to be hard-wired into a vehicle are now available. Instead, the FM modulator simply sends a wireless signal to the FM tuner, and it's picked up as a radio station. Wired FM modulators provide superior sound quality, however.

FM modulators offer a quick, easy, and inexpensive way to integrate an iPod into an existing car stereo, whether stock or aftermarket. A variety of aftermarket FM modulator products are available, ranging from simple to complex. Most will also charge your iPod at the same time. But FM modulators have two major drawbacks:

- Your music will only sound as good as the best FM reception, which is way below CD quality.

- If you live in or you're passing through an urban area, it can be hard to find an empty spot on the FM dial, and even if you do, you can easily get interference from adjacent stations.

It's a good idea to look for an FM modulator what allows you to select from a variety of FM frequencies, such as Monster Cable's iCarPlay Wireless Plus, shown in Figure 7-1. That way, if one FM frequency is occupied or filled with static, you can tune to another one.

Testing, testing . . .

Here's a good test to determine the quality of the FM modulator for your iPod (or any other MP3 player). Connect the MP3 player to the FM modulator and find a blank station on the FM dial for the signal. Then pause the iPod, turn radio all the way up, turn on the car's engine, headlights, and rev the engine and listen for noise. A high-quality FM modulator is relatively quiet, whereas a low-quality one produces more noise.

Figure 7-1:
Monster
Cable's
iCarPlay
Wireless
Plus sends
an iPod's
signal to an
existing car
stereo.

Aftermarket head units

Full iPod integration in an aftermarket head unit offers much better sound quality than FM modulators because the audio signal is fed directly into the head unit. And it also allows easy access to the music on the iPod through the head unit's own controls and provides information on the head unit's display. This way, you never have to touch your iPod after you hook it up to a head unit, which is a huge safety advantage as well as a major convenience.

But not all iPod–ready head units are created equal. Most offer basic controls that allow accessing music just as you would on an iPod: by artists, albums, songs, and playlists. And the head unit displays the corresponding info visually. One of the biggest factors you should think about when considering iPod integration is access speed.

Alpine, for example, advertises its latest-generation iPod integration products as *full speed,* meaning that the rate at which you can access tunes on an iPod via one of the company's head units (see Figure 7-2) is about the same as if you were operating the iPod itself. Kenwood, Pioneer, and Clarion also offer high-speed iPod access. Plus, most head units with iPod integration also charge the device while it's connected.

Figure 7-2:
Alpine's
CDA-9883
offers *full
speed*
access to
music on an
iPod.

Courtesy of Alpine Electronics

Aftermarket iPod adaptors

Leave it to the car audio aftermarket to give the people what they want. These days, what people want is to use their iPods while they're on the road, no matter what car they drive or whether they have an aftermarket head unit. Some people may not be willing or even able to change out their radios because of cosmetic or cost concerns or lease restrictions. That's where innovative car audio accessory companies such as Blitzsafe, PAC, Peripheral, PIE, and Scosche have come to the rescue.

Such companies may not be household names or even have the marquee value of other large and well-known car audio brands, but they are renowned in the car audio industry for providing solutions, largely to car audio specialty dealers, that integrate aftermarket electronics into almost any kind of vehicle. In the case of iPod integration, these companies offer adaptors that tap into a vehicle's factory wiring and electronics so that the popular music player can be added without high costs or hassles.

Scosche's AXIPTA, for example (see Figure 7-3), fits many 2004 and up Toyota, Scion, and Lexus vehicles and allows control of an iPod from the stock head unit, which also displays all of the control and track info. Such adaptors are also non-invasive, meaning they can be taken out and the car can be returned to stock condition.

Figure 7-3:
Scosche's
AXIPTA
allows
adding iPod
control to
many 2004
and up
Toyota,
Scion, and
Lexus
vehicles.

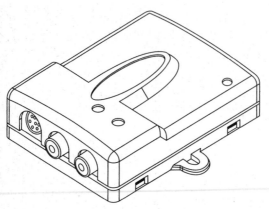

Courtesy of Schosche

Auxiliary inputs

Auxiliary inputs designed for plugging in a separate audio source have been around a long time, and they usually pop up like mushrooms after a rain storm when a new audio format comes on the scene. They were somewhat prevalent when CDs were still rare in car audio, for example, and people wanted to a plug a portable CD player into their car's cassette-based head unit. A car audio system I put together in the late 1980s, for example, had an aux-in on the back of the head unit, into which I plugged a portable CD.

Today, many aftermarket car audio head units sport aux inputs, as do an increasing percentage of new cars. Car manufacturers have recognized this as a feature that more and more consumers want. Although most are 3.5mm *miniplug* jacks (see Figure 7-4), which fit the same connector that an iPod and other MP3 player use, a few use RCA-based aux inputs like those found on most car and home audio components (see Figure 7-5).

An aux-in jack is an easy and affordable way to jack an iPod (or any MP3 player or auxiliary audio source) into a car audio system, but you still have to fumble with the device to control it, which isn't very convenient or safe while behind the wheel. And it's not iPod-specific, which means you can plug in any outboard audio device.

Figure 7-4: A *miniplug* 3.5mm auxiliary-input jack in a Nissan Xterra.

Figure 7-5: RCA aux-in jacks in an Infiniti M35x.

Some car audio companies that don't make head units have also gotten in on the aux-in act. They allow an iPod or other MP3 player to be added into a system's signal chain on an amplifier, equalizer, or some other component (see Figure 7-6).

Figure 7-6:
Blaupunkt's
GTA 480
amplifier
has an aux
input.

Courtesy of Blaupunkt

Car dealer kits

BMW launched the first iPod integration application among carmakers in mid-2004, with a dealer-installed option that allowed owners of certain Bimmer models to control the device via steering-wheel audio controls. Information such as artist, album, and song can be displayed on the in-dash head unit. Since that time, fourteen more auto manufacturers have begun offering iPod integration kits. (You can see a complete and updated list at www.apple.com/ipod/carintegration.html.) The obvious advantage of this approach to iPod integration is that you can keep a factory look.

Sync and the future

As the iPod becomes more entrenched and widespread and other portable players come on the scene to challenge its dominance, look for more car-integration solutions to appear. Ford recently unveiled its Sync system, for example, which was developed in conjunction with Microsoft. It allows complete control of a portable music player via voice commands and steering-wheel switches, as well as cool features such as a "play similar" command that will automatically cull a playlist based on your music preferences.

USB in the Dash

An MP3 player syncs to Ford's Sync via a USB port, which has become as common as clover on all sorts of electronic products. Originally found on computers, USB (which stands for Universal Serial Bus) has quickly migrated to all sorts of electronics products as a quick way to transfer information. Now car audio systems, both aftermarket and stock, are beginning to sport USB ports.

Another way in for the iPod

One of the primary applications for USB drives in cars has been as a way to integrate an iPod. Because it's also the way an iPod syncs to your computer, a USB connection provides the best possible sound quality as well as slightly faster access to music on an iPod. Consequently, most of the major car audio manufacturers that offer iPod integration use a USB connection to dock an iPod and transfer information to and from the device.

Thumb drives

Car audio head units have also begun to sprout USB drives on their front panels (see Figure 7-7). This allows easy and quick access to digital music files loaded on a USB *thumb* drive, a small flash-memory device that is about the size of a person's thumb. Depending on the capacity of the USB drive (which is measured in megabytes or gigabytes, with higher being better), it's possible to store dozens of songs on a drive small enough to fit in your pocket.

Figure 7-7:
A Kenwood head unit with a USB port and a thumb drive attached.

Courtesy of Kenwood

In the Cards: SD and MMC

Yet another way to carry MP3 files on the road is with Secure Digital (SD) and MultiMediaCards (MMC). You're probably familiar with these if you own a digital camera because many use the removable cards to store pictures. As with USB drives, the larger the capacity of the SD or MMC cards, the more tunes you can store on it, and the more expensive the card is. And because they are even smaller than USB drives, SD and MMC cards are a convenient way to carry dozens of MP3s on the road.

SD and MMC cards actually predate the presence of USB drives in the car audio world by several years, and SD cards have proven to be the dominant format. A few manufacturers — including Clarion, Dual, and Jensen — now offer SD card slots on their head units, typically behind a fold-down faceplate. And Audi, Mercedes, and Honda offer SD card slots in the dash on the OEM side.

Hard Disc Drives: Burn, Baby, Burn

Higher-capacity iPods and similar MP3 players are simply data storage devices with functions that allow you to access your tunes, whereas USB drives and SD cards are simply flash drives for temporarily storing your music files. But chances are you also store all of your tunes on your computer's hard drive and transfer it over to a hard-disc MP3 player or flash-memory device.

So why not install a hard-disc drive (HDD) into your car and just dump all of your tunes on it? Well, several car audio manufacturers had the same idea a few years ago, about the time the whole iPod craze kicked in. But by that time, most people didn't want to go through the hassle of downloading their music to a hard drive in the car, which involved the tedious task of ripping songs from CDs one disc at a time, when they could have all the music on their iPod or other MP3 player. Subsequently, HDD head units never really caught on. There are still some around (like the Alpine HDA-5460 shown in Figure 7-8), and you can probably get a killer deal on one.

Some high-end head units these days use an HDD for the mapping database and operating system for GPS navigation because it offers fast access time. Pioneer and Eclipse (see Figure 7-9) also offer nav-based head units with an HDD, with part of the disc space used for storing music.

Courtesy of Alpine Electronics

Figure 7-8: Alpine's HAD-5460 contains a hard-disc drive for storing music files.

Figure 7-9: The Eclipse AVN5495 has a hard-disc drive that's used for navigation as well as storing music files.

Courtesy of Eclipse Electronics

The HDD has also found a home in some stock car audio systems. Cars from Cadillac, Chrysler, Dodge, Infiniti, and Lexus offer in-dash HDDs for storing hundreds of digital music files.

Chapter 8

The Golden Age of Wireless

*T*he very first entertainment technology to hit the road was radio — and for years it was the only one. AM and later FM provided music, news, weather, and other info to enhance cruising around town and to break the boredom of a long road trip. After other formats began to allow drivers to listen to what they wanted instead of what the DJ wanted to play, radio lost some of its supremacy as king of the road.

But in the last few years, modern technology has breathed new life into this age-old format. Satellite radio offers CD-quality sound and hundreds of commercial-free channels of music, news, sports, weather, traffic, and more. HD Radio also has CD-quality sound and *hidden* sub-frequencies that offer alternative, largely commercial-free programming. Plus, unlike satellite radio, HD radio is free.

And there's a new wireless technology increasingly creeping into cars: Bluetooth. Originally designed for hands-free mobile phone use behind the wheel, Bluetooth's Advanced Audio Distribution Profile (A2DP) promises to issue in a new era in wireless entertainment.

In this chapter, I delve into the latest in radio, including satellite and HD Radio, and how you can get it into your car. I also take a look at how Bluetooth is expanding from mobile phone to mobile music applications and what it means to the car audio enthusiast.

Music of the Spheres: Satellite Radio

The introduction of satellite radio in the early part of the twenty-first century was the most significant change to the medium since FM became popular in the 1970s. It was also the first time people were asked to pay for radio, which up until that time been free.

Analogies were made to the launch of cable TV in the 1970s, which has since proved to be wildly popular. Although satellite radio hasn't experienced the pervasive popularity of cable TV, it has changed the way people think about radio and what the medium can offer — and racked up millions of subscribers in the process. And satellite radio makes a lot of sense for the car: Besides entertainment programming and news, the service can also provide up-to-the-minute and accurate traffic information.

XM Satellite Radio (see Figure 8-1) launched in late 2001, offering 100 channels of basic programming for $9.99 per month. Sirius Satellite Radio (see Figure 8-2) entered service about six months later, with a basic subscription charge of $12.95 per month and the same number of channels. (XM now charges $12.95/month for 175 channels and Sirius the same for more than 130 channels.)

Figure 8-1:
XM Satellite
Radio's logo.

Courtesy of XM Satellite Radio

Figure 8-2:
Sirius
Satellite
Radio's logo.

Courtesy of Sirius Satellite Radio

Soon after these companies were born, aftermarket car audio companies began siding with one satellite radio provider or the other to offer tuners that could receive the service. XM and Sirius also aligned with car companies as part of their marketing plans to take the service mainstream.

XM has since partnered with Acura, Buick, Cadillac, Chevrolet, Ferrari, GMC, Honda, Hummer, Hyundai, Infiniti, Isuzu, Lexus, Lotus, Nissan, Pontiac, Porsche, Saab, Saturn, Scion, Subaru, Suzuki, and Toyota. Sirius has linked with Audi, Bentley, BMW, Chrysler, Dodge, Ford, Infiniti, Jaguar, Jeep, Land Rover, Lexus, Lincoln BMW, Maybach, Mazda, Mercedes, MINI, Mitsubishi, Nissan, Scion, Subaru, Toyota, Volkswagen, and Volvo.

Both companies offer a free trial period for buyers of new cars equipped with their respective services, hoping that after these drivers have a taste of satellite radio, they'll continue with their subscriptions. According to industry sources, the *take* rate on continued subscriptions has been a little more than 50 percent.

But the car audio aftermarket is the source for adding satellite radio to an existing car or system, and there have never been more options for getting the service. Plus, more car audio companies have become non-partisan towards satellite radio and now offer ways to get either or both services using their equipment. For example, some of Alpine and Pioneer CD head units can now tune in one or both services.

Plus, when satellite radio was first introduced, a bulky tuner box and a large, unsightly antenna was needed to access the service. But today, the tuners are often built into a head unit with the addition of a tiny chip, and antennas have shrunk significantly as well. Plus, there are numerous portable options that can be easily added to a vehicle's sound system. For example, both XM and Sirius offer portable radios that you can use anywhere, just like an MP3 player (in fact, some have built-in MP3 players) in a home while docked into an entertainment system, or anywhere else while docked in boom box. These portables can be integrated into a vehicle as well.

In the latest development, the two satellite radio companies, XM and Sirius, are seeking to merge to form one company, pending government approval. Regardless of the outcome, satellite radio is yet another way that the modern car audio enthusiast can enjoy hours and hours of great music, entertainment, news, weather, sports, and traffic info behind the wheel.

What's the Frequency, Kenneth?: HD Radio

HD Radio (see Figure 8-3) probably would have come to pass even if satellite radio didn't begin to pose a threat to traditional terrestrial or land-based broadcasters. But from the beginning, HD Radio was heavily promoted as a "free" alternative to satellite radio. The mobile-music listener is the real winner in the radio wars because it all boils down to better sound and more choices for in-car listening.

Courtesy of HD Radio

What HD Radio is

With HD Radio, a digital signal *piggybacks* onto regular analog radio broad-casts. Because the HD Radio signal is digital, FM can potentially sound as good as a CD and AM as good as FM. Plus, there's virtually no static, drop-offs, hiss, or the other noises or reception problems associated with analog radio broadcast.

An HD Radio station can also offer *multicasting,* meaning it can broadcast sepa-rate programming on a sub-frequency of its allotted spot on the dial, which can only be picked up by an HD tuner. Most stations use the sub-frequencies to broadcast largely commercial-free programming that's much like satellite radio. For example, a country station in Portland, Oregon provides a sub-frequency that broadcasts blues programming, whereas a smooth jazz station in Miami offers classical music as its multicasting option.

Another advantage of HD Radio is that information such as artist name and song title as well as weather and traffic alerts and even stock quotes can be sent with a signal and shown on the radio's display. And HD Radio promises to provide many other features in the future, including

- Real-time traffic reports
- Surround sound
- Store-and-replay functions that allow rewinding a song or even recording an entire program to play back later
- On-demand news and information
- *Buy* buttons that allow purchasing everything from music to products advertised on a station

Where you can get it

HD Radio is available in the top 100 media markets in the U.S. and in 188 markets altogether. For a listing of the stations that carry HD programming, go to www.hdradio.com on the Web.

How you can get it

Alpine, Eclipse, JVC, Kenwood, Panasonic, and Sony offer aftermarket HD Radio products. Some have HD Radio built into their head units, whereas others allow you to add it to a head unit with the addition of an extra-cost tuner box. Directed Electronics' Car Connect HD Radio (see Figure 8-4) is a tuner and display/controller with an FM modulator that can be added to any vehicle. Automotive electronics supplier Visteon also offers two add-on options. So far, only BMW offers HD Radio as a factory-installed option on the OEM side, but Jaguar, Mini, and Hyundai will offer it on 2008 models.

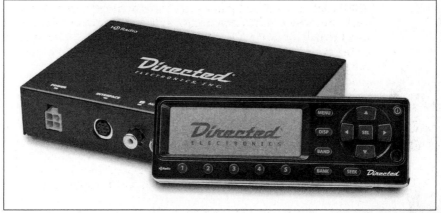

Figure 8-4:
Directed Electronics' Car Connect HD Radio tuner can be connected to any existing car radio.

Courtesy of Directed Electronics

Linking in with Bluetooth

You've probably heard the term *Bluetooth* and may even know what it means. But you probably didn't know that it was named after a medieval Scandinavian king who reportedly had a penchant for eating blueberries.

Bluetooth is the strange name (coined by the Swedish mobile phone company, Erricson, which developed the technology) for technology that uses a short-range network to wirelessly connect electronic components. It's been a huge hit in the mobile-phone market because it allows hands-free operation. You probably best know it from people you see walking around with those futuristic-looking headsets, seemingly talking to themselves. But it has expanded into everything from computer printers to photo frames that display digital pictures.

But it's in the car for hands-free mobile phone use that Bluetooth has really caught on with consumers because it's a natural for safe mobile-phone use behind the wheel. But in some states it's more of a requirement than a convenience if you want to talk while driving. At the time of this writing, Connecticut, New Jersey, Utah, Washington, and California (starting in July 2008) have all banned handheld phone use by a driver. Washington, D.C. has also outlawed drivers yakking on handheld cell phones, as have many municipalities. More are sure to follow, which bodes well for Bluetooth.

Bluetooth head units

With more mobile phones including Bluetooth these days, it's become standard equipment or an option on many new cars. It's also a popular add-on car accessory. Aftermarket Bluetooth kits that add hands-free mobile phone capability to a car range from simple plug-and-play kits that can move from vehicle to vehicle, to fully wired applications that automatically mute a car's audio system when a call comes in and plays the call over the car's speakers (see Figure 8-5).

Figure 8-5:
Parrot's
MK6100
Bluetooth kit
will
automati-
cally
answer a
call and has
A2DP
capability.

Courtesy of Parrot

Bluetooth is also increasingly available as a feature on many car audio head units. It can either be added on via a separate adaptor or built-in. Bluetooth is now available in high- to middle-end car audio head units, but the feature will eventually trickle down to lower-priced head units (see Figure 8-6).

Figure 8-6:
Parrot's
RK8200 is a
car audio
head unit
with
Bluetooth
built in.

Courtesy of Parrot

 But Bluetooth isn't just for phones anymore. Several accessories manufacturers offer products that allow adding Bluetooth wireless capability to iPods and other MP3 players so that they can play over aftermarket and even stock car audio systems.

Bluetooth A2DP

As more Bluetooth mobile phones, PDAs, and smart phones double as music players (such as Motorola ROKR with iTunes built in), and more MP3 players begin to incorporate Bluetooth, the technology is poised to break into the music business. That's if A2DP catches on with consumers, which allows music from a compatible device to be sent wirelessly to an A2DP-compatible stereo receiver.

Wireless Bluetooth speakers for home stereos with A2DP technology have started to appear, and now car stereos are starting to cut the cord as well. The latest Bluetooth head units from Pioneer (Figure 8-7) have built-in A2DP capability, which allows for hands-free phone use as well as wireless streaming of music from an A2DP device. This could be just the beginning of a larger trend because more people are bringing phones and portable media players (PMPs) — or a combination of the two — into their vehicles, and Bluetooth is catching on like wildfire. If these trends continue, and they should, expect to see A2DP become more widespread, offering the ability to cut the cord between a car stereo and a PMP or a mobile phone/MP3 player with A2DP onboard.

Figure 8-7:
Pioneer's
Premier
DEH-
P790BT
offers built
in Bluetooth
capability
with A2DP
music
streaming.

Courtesy of Pioneer

Chapter 9

Moving Pictures

· ·

· ·

I remember back in the 1970s, while I was at a Little League baseball game one evening, a friend had a small black-and-white TV in his dad's car that was powered by a cigarette lighter and connected to a small antenna clipped to one of the car's windows. It also happened to be the night of the Major League Baseball All-Star game and a bunch of people stood around the car watching it on the little B&W set.

The crowd around the car grew to the point where someone suggested that the TV be turned off because the audience for the game on the screen was larger than the one for the game on the field! My friend's dad's response was to crank up the car and drive away. I still remember the bluish light from that little B&W TV in the backseat as they drove away. At the time, that was state-of-the-art in mobile video, but now it seems as quaint as eight-track tapes.

Today, you have many different options for watching movies on the road, thanks to the advent of the DVD. In this chapter, I cover all of your options for getting the show on the road. I look at the DVD-based system in every permutation and at which features are most important. I also discuss portable options and videogaming on the go.

Drivin' Movies

Today, you can not only watch almost anything you want in a vehicle — in color and with surround sound — and even have separate screens showing separate programming, with wireless headphones that allow passengers to listen to the audio without disturbing others in the vehicle.

Starting in the late 1990s, mobile video became a dominant force in the car audio aftermarket, which had a lot to do with the advent of the DVD player. Although there were videocassette players and video monitors available for cars before the introduction of the DVD, it took the ability to bring movies and other entertainment into the car on a small shiny disc to kick-start the mobile-video craze. Although mobile video is still dominated by DVD, today you can get mobile video into your vehicle in a variety of ways, including on hard drives and via satellite.

And there's a huge array of choices in video screens — everything from stand-alone monitors that you can mount anywhere to complete video console systems that include a screen, a DVD player, wireless headphones, and more. You can even get systems that allow you to add mobile video without permanently altering your vehicle. Basically, you'll find a system to fit every car and budget.

In-Dash DVD Players

When car DVD players first appeared on the scene, they were expensive, but through the miracle of consumer electronics, prices have steadily dropped in the decade since the first DVD players appeared. In fact, you can now get a budget-priced DVD-based head unit for about the price you'd pay for high-quality CD head unit. Name-brand in-dash DVD receivers can be had for as low as $200. Apart from budget, your main concern when shopping for a DVD player should be deciding which configuration will work with your particular vehicle and needs. In the next few section, I cover the options.

Double-DIN head units

Think of double-DIN units as *super-sized* head units. DIN stands for Deutsches Institute für Normung, which in English translates to "German Institute for Standardization." It's simply a worldwide standard, which in this case refers to the size of a typical in-dash radio: 2 inches high, 7 inches wide, and 7 inches deep. Double-DIN simply means that the head unit is twice the height of a single-DIN unit, 4 inches high, and is meant to fit a corresponding stock opening in the dash (see Figure 9-1).

Car makes that have double-DIN openings include Ford, GM, and Toyota. If you want a double-DIN head unit in your dash and you only have a single-DIN stock opening, you can always modify your dash to make it fit. But you could be facing a lot of expensive and time-consuming modification in the process.

The main advantage of a double-DIN DVD head unit is that it has more front-panel real estate for a large screen, as well as more area for buttons and controls. And most head units have fixed screens, whereas single-DIN audio/video head units usually have a screen that folds out of the unit via motorization, which are more prone to failure and can block air vents, controls, or other parts of a vehicle.

Double the DIN, double the functions

Some double-DIN DVD heads double as navigation systems and even have separate DVD slots for navigation and entertainment, such as the Eclipse's AVN6610, shown in the following figure. This makes it easier to switch out navigation DVDs directly from the head unit, as opposed to in the trunk or under a front seat for an outboard nav system. (This isn't much of an advantage if you have one of the latest DVD navigation systems that includes navigation mapping for the entire U.S. on a single DVD: You never have to go to the trouble of switching those discs unless you leave the United States anyway.) But the biggest advantage to having the nav system built into a DVD head unit

is that it's less costly and complicated to install compared to a system that uses a separate DVD navigation drive.

Other double-DIN DVD heads, such as Eclipse's AVN5495 and Pioneer's AVIC-Z2, shown in the following figure, include navigation systems that use a hard disk drive (HDD) for storage of operating and mapping software. This provides even faster response times than DVD-based nav systems that are integrated into a head unit. And these two HDD units also use part of the hard disk space for music storage.

(continued)

(continued)

Fold-out screens

Single-DIN DVD head units don't have room for a large screen on their front panels, so many use a motorized fold-out screen. At the press of a button, the screen slides out of the head unit, as shown in Figure 9-2. Press again and it folds in.

Although the motorized screen saves space, they are typically more expensive than a comparable double-DIN DVD head. Plus, they are also more prone to malfunctioning due to their extra complexity. Ask friends or check Internet forums such as www.sounddomain.com for single-DIN DVD players with fold-out screens that are reliable and less prone to malfunctioning.

All in-dash DVD players with a built-in screen are sold with a *lock-out* circuit that prevents video from playing on the screen while the vehicle is in motion. These are usually tied to the parking brake or a navigation system. This is included as a safety precaution to prevent drivers from watching a movie when they should be watching the road.

Unscrupulous installers and DIYers have devised ways to circumvent such circuits, but putting lives at risk on the road so that you can watch a video just isn't worth it. Save it for the backseat or when the car is parked. Plus, it's against the law to have a video screen within view of a driver in all 50 states, with the exception of using it for navigation purposes.

Figure 9-1:
Kenwood's
DDX8019 is
an example
of a double-
DIN head
unit.

Figure 9-2:
A 6.5-inch
screen
slides out of
the Alpine
IVA-D105
DVD head
unit.

Players only

Some in-dash DVD players don't have built-in screens, but can send a video signal out to a monitor or monitors elsewhere in a vehicle. Many single-DIN in-dash DVD players without a screen have what's known as *dual zone* capability, which I explain later in the chapter. And some in-dash single-DIN DVD players have small screens, such as Jensen's VM8012 (see Figure 9-3).

Figure 9-3:
Jensen's
VM8012 is a
single-DIN
head unit
with a 3-
inch screen.

Courtesy of Jensen

Keep in mind that DVD players can also play CDs, but not the other way around. Plus, most DVD players can also play MP3 and WMA music files, control an iPod, and receive USB input. But the main reason to buy a DVD head unit is, of course, for its video capabilities.

DVD-Audio

DVD-Audio is a high-resolution, multichannel music format that was introduced a couple of years after the DVD-Video made its debut in 1997. In the same way that DVD-Video made watching movies on videocassette effectively obsolete, DVD-Audio initially promised to do the same to CD.

But unlike its phenomenally popular predecessor, DVD-Audio never caught on with consumers and was never fully supported by the music industry. Plus, it came out just before the iPod took off, and most people were more concerned with the quantity of tunes they could bring into the car rather than their sound quality.

Although DVD-Audio is still a staple in high-end stock audio systems in some luxury cars, the format is all but dead in the aftermarket. Only Alpine and Pioneer currently offer DVD-Audio head units in the aftermarket, and they are both run more than $2,000 as of this writing.

If you can find (and afford) an aftermarket DVD-Audio head unit for your car, it'll give you the best of both worlds because you can also play DVD-Video discs (although DVD-Video players can't play DVD-Audio discs). But you'll also need a 5.1 surround-sound system with two front channels, a center channel, two rear surround channels, and a subwoofer in order to make the most of the format's multichannel capabilities.

DVD Head Unit Features

DVD head units have many features that overlap those of a CD head unit, so in the following sections I detailed features that are exclusive to DVD heads. (For more on CD head unit features, flip to the next chapter, Chapter 10.

Dual-zone capability

This is the ability to send signals to two separate entertainment *zones* within a vehicle. A dual-zone head, for example, can send a video signal from a DVD to a screen or screens in the rear of the vehicle, while the audio signal is sent to wireless infrared headphones. This allows a vehicle to have two separate entertainment zones: one in the front and one in the back. For example, while backseat passengers are watching a DVD on separate screens and listening to the DVD on headphones, the driver and front-seat passenger can be listening to FM or satellite radio though the speakers in the vehicle.

Video output

A video output is an jack on the back of a DVD head unit that allows you to hook up extra screens. The video signal is taken out of the head unit, for example, and sent to screens elsewhere in the vehicle.

Auxiliary audio/video inputs

Auxiliary inputs allow you to add an external audio or video source, such as a videogame console or portable media player. In this way, for example, those in the front seat can listen to a CD while those in the back play videogames or watch programming from a portable DVD player or a portable media player. Some newer systems even allow hooking up a video iPod.

DVD Beyond the Dash

There are many more ways to get video into your vehicle than adding a DVD head unit, although they are primarily for backseat-viewing purposes. And some of these can be much more affordable and practical than building a car video system from scratch around an in-dash DVD player.

Headrest monitors/DVD players

In the early days of car video, a headrest monitor was a custom-installed item that required hours of labor because installers had to mount screens in headrests by hand. Today, however, you can buy a headrest with a video screen and even a DVD player already imbedded in it that not only fits your vehicle, but also perfectly matches the upholstery.

All-in-one headrest systems have become a particularly popular option for people who only want to add backseat video to their vehicles and not a full-blown car audio/video system. VizuaLogic, for example, offers headrests systems (shown in Figure 9-4) that fit more than 7,000 vehicles. They also install easily, with no permanent modification to the vehicle, and they can be taken out when the vehicle is sold or the lease is up. Such systems come in one of two configurations:

- ✔ Two headrests, each with a screen, and one with a DVD player that is shared by both screens.
- ✔ Two headrests, each with its own DVD player.

Many headrest DVD video systems also come with an FM modulator so that audio from a DVD can be played over a vehicle's existing audio system, and wireless infrared headphones can be added for private listening. Some systems also allow jacking in iPod video or music or media from other MP3 and portable media players.

Overhead video consoles

An overhead video console is another popular video add-on option in the form of an all-in-one console that can be attached to the ceiling of a vehicle (see Figure 9-5). An overhead video console usually contains a screen, a DVD player, an infrared transmitter, and wireless headphones. Some even have separate screens and dual DVD players so that backseat passengers can enjoy separate movies (see Figure 9-6).

Figure 9-4:
This
VizuaLogic
headrest
DVD system
fits the 2007
Ford Edge.

Courtesy of VizuaLogic

Figure 9-5:
Audiovox's
VDO122 is a
ceiling
console
with a DVD
player and
12.2-inch
screen.

Courtesy of Audiovox

Figure 9-6:
The Advent ADV285 comes with two 8.5-inch screens and two DVD players.

Raw monitors

You can also buy a *raw* standalone monitor (Figure 9-7) and mount it anywhere you want. Although this offers the most flexibility and a custom look, it also requires a lot of labor — either your own or a custom installer's.

As the name implies, a standalone monitor has to be tied to another component, such as a head unit, in order to play video. But the latest products from Alpine and Kenwood allow you to plug an iPod video into a standalone monitor.

There's a whole slew of stand-alone video monitors available, in all sizes and price ranges, so you'll be able to find one that works for just about any application you can dream up. But there's an equally wide range of quality — and you get what you pay for. So it's wise to stick with a reputable brand that will stand behind its products.

Portable options

With all of the portable video systems available, going this route can also make sense for your car video needs. But you want to make sure a portable doesn't become a UFO (unsecured flying object) in case of an accident. A variety of portables that attach to a seat or center console are available specifically for the car. These *video-in-a-bag* products can then be unattached and moved to another vehicle (Figure 9-8).

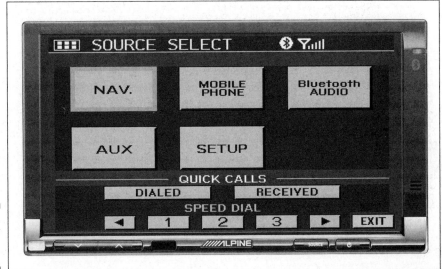

Figure 9-7:
An Alpine
raw monitor.

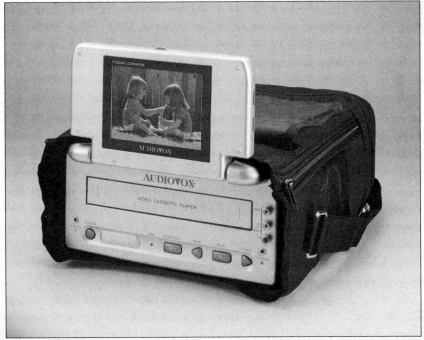

Figure 9-8:
An
Audiovox
video-in-a-
bag product.

Other portables offer more flexibility — and more places where they can be used. Audiovox's DVD Shuttle System (Figure 9-9) consists of a series of portable players with screen sizes of 7, 8.5, or 10.2 inches that can be popped into optional dock stations for the car or home.

Directed Electronics' Portable Entertainment System (Figure 9-10) combines a portable DVD player with a docking station that mounts on the ceiling of a vehicle. The docking station also houses a slot for an optional digital-video recorder (DVR) that can store hours of video. And the same slot also accommodates a video iPod.

Videogaming on the Go

Videogames can also keep backseat occupants occupied for miles. Although there are plenty of handheld videogame solutions, they don't allow head-to-head competition. (I still haven't decided whether this is a good thing or a bad thing.) Many car audio/video systems can easily be upgraded with an A/V aux-in jack that allows you to add in a videogame console, or any other A/V source for that matter. Even some stock stereo systems have this feature, as well as a 110-volt outlet for powering a videogame console (Figure 9-11).

Figure 9-9:
Audiovox's DVD Shuttle System makes it easy to move a screen and DVD player between vehicles.

Courtesy of Audiovox

Figure 9-10:
Directed
Electronics'
Portable
Entertain-
ment
System
docks into
a ceiling
mount.

Courtesy of Directed Electronics

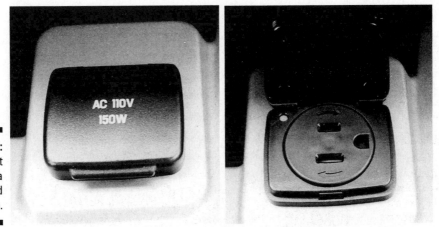

Figure 9-11:
A 110-volt
outlet in a
Ford
Escape.

It isn't that expensive to have a shop add a 110-volt inverter to your car, and handy DIYers can handle the job on their own. Finally, several aftermarket video-component suppliers have even started to package videogame systems with their product offerings as a value-added feature.